WANTING MORE OF GOD

How to attain to the fullness of Christ

Mark & Fiona Gilpin

Copyright © 2025 Mark and Fiona Gilpin. All rights reserved.
First published in Great Britain by Evangelism Reimagined, 2025.

No part of this book shall be reproduced or transmitted in any form or by any means, electronic or mechanical, including photocopying, recording, or by any information retrieval system without prior written permission of the copyright owner except as permitted under the Copyright, Designs and Patents Act 1988.

Evangelism Reimagined
www.evangelismreimagined.org
ISBN 978-1-7390995-5-8

A Catalogue record for this book is available from the British Library.

Produced by Evangelism Reimagined Publishing
info@evangelismreimagined.org
Printed and bound in Great Britain

This book is sold subject to the condition that it shall not, by way of trade or otherwise, be lent, resold, hired out or otherwise circulated without the publisher's prior written consent in any form of binding or cover other than that in which it is published and without a similar condition including this condition being imposed on the subsequent purchaser.

Scriptures quoted are from the NIV unless otherwise stated.
Scripture quotations are taken from THE HOLY BIBLE, NEW INTERNATIONAL VERSION®, NIV® Copyright © 1973, 1978, 1984, 2011 by Biblica, Inc.™
Used by permission. All rights reserved worldwide.

Permission was obtained from the Evangelical Alliance to use the Engel Scale diagram.

Strong's Definitions are referenced from www.blueletterbible.org.

Some names and identifying details in our stories have been changed to protect the privacy of individuals mentioned in this work.

The websites cited in this book are offered solely as a resource to the reader. The citation of these websites does not in any way imply an endorsement on the part of the authors or the publisher, nor does the authors or publisher vouch for their content for the life of this book.

ABOUT THE AUTHORS

Mark and Fiona Gilpin are authors, speakers and evangelists who equip Christians to freely enjoy evangelism. They founded Evangelism Reimagined, an evangelism training ministry, which transforms people's experience of evangelism, making it accessible to all Christians.[1]

They are both passionate about enabling others to freely enjoy speaking about Jesus confidently and courageously. They create an environment where evangelism is fun and adventurous, without guilt, shame, or condemnation.

They empower Christians into a Spirit-led lifestyle, where God can invite them into an evangelistic moment at any time, any place, anywhere. Mark and Fiona have trained churches and Christians in evangelism for over twenty-five years.

Mark helps people discover a motivation for evangelism and how we have all been designed to be evangelistic. Fiona helps people find freedom from negative experiences of evangelism, overcome fear, and embrace the adventure that evangelism is meant to be.

They both love to bring the reality of the Kingdom of God to unbelievers wherever they are. They bring confidence to Spirit-

---

[1] Evangelism Reimagined. https://www.evangelismreimagined.org

led evangelism and a way of introducing people to Jesus that creates a desire for more.

Mark and Fiona created the *Developing a Spirit-led Evangelistic Lifestyle (DASEL)* training course, which helps churches and individuals to reimagine evangelism and develop an evangelistic culture and lifestyle.

They are also authors of the book *God's Dream: Our Greatest Privilege*, which helps people overcome their hindrances to evangelism and takes them on a journey to discover the purpose God has for them in fulfilling his dream.

To all those seeking more of God

The Spirit of the Sovereign Lord is on me,
because the Lord has anointed me
to proclaim good news to the poor.

He has sent me to bind up the broken-hearted,
to proclaim freedom for the captives
and release from darkness for the prisoners,
to proclaim the year of the Lord's favour
and the day of vengeance of our God,
to comfort all who mourn,
and provide for those who grieve in Zion –
to bestow on them a crown of beauty
instead of ashes,
the oil of joy
instead of mourning,
and a garment of praise
instead of a spirit of despair.

They will be called oaks of righteousness,
a planting of the Lord
for the display of his splendour.

Isaiah 61:1-3

*To be filled with God is a great thing,
to be filled with the fullness of God is still greater;
to be filled with all the fullness of God is greatest of all.*

Adam Clarke
(Theologian & Biblical Scholar)

CONTENTS

FOREWORD xiii
PREFACE xv
ACKNOWLEDGEMENTS xix
ENDORSEMENTS xxi
PART ONE REMOVING CLUTTER 1
    MAKING SPACE FOR JESUS 3
    DO NOT WORRY 17
    BE QUICK TO FORGIVE 37
    DO NOT BE DISMAYED 55
    KNOW YOU ARE WONDERFULLY MADE 77
    BE PATIENT IN AFFLICTION 95
PART TWO FINDING JESUS 121
    WHERE IS JESUS? 123
    JESUS IN THE BIBLE 139
    JESUS IN THE CHURCH 163
    JESUS IN US 189
    JESUS AMONG THE LOST 211
    JESUS AMONG THE MARGINALISED 243
    REMAINING IN JESUS 269

FOREWORD

People are hungry for God, both in the church and in the wider world. Those who have tasted a little of God's goodness often begin a journey into his fullness – to know and experience him more. The apostle Paul wrote to a group of believers in Colosse and told them to avoid trying to find meaning and life in human philosophy and tradition because:

"*For in Christ all the fullness of the Deity lives in bodily form, 10 and in Christ you have been brought to fullness. He is the head over every power and authority.*" (Col 2:9,10). Knowing more of God's fullness is the inheritance of every Christian and the goal of our discipleship – it is both given and attained. How so?

That is the grand subject of Mark and Fiona's excellent book. Let them take you on a journey to discover more of God's fullness in Christ. This amazing couple have lived and breathed this journey together as disciples, parents and as evangelists, whose supreme joy is to share Jesus' fullness, and teach others to do the same.

It is rare to find evangelists inspiring us in an area which is often the preserve of pastors and teachers – our growth into maturity in Christ. But this book is a prophetic call to combine love for God with love for the lost, a hunger for more of his fullness with a passion for those who don't know him yet.

So often separated in our thinking and experience, in the life of Jesus they never were, as he loved the Father (and the Father loved him) and reached the fatherless, the marginalised and the disadvantaged. Reading their stories I was moved by their lives, fashioned as they are by joyful sharing, patience in affliction, and abundant fruit.

I have sat with them in the places where Jesus can be found, seen them move in love and miracles, and inspire others to do the same. I can only encourage you to go on the journey with them as you read this book and reflect on the beautiful saviour they know and love. Learn with them how to encounter God more deeply and discover more of his fullness among the lost, the poor and the needy.

You will be changed, and so will your world.

David Webster M.A.
Author of *Your Royal Identity* and the *Edison Series* of children's books.

PREFACE

*I just want more, more of you, God.
To receive, not in part but the fullness of who you are.*
(More, Red Rocks Worship)

The heart cry and prayer of many Christians today is that they want more of God. Maybe that is you. How many times have you asked God for more? How many times in sung worship have you poured out your heart and soul asking for more or prayed out loud the phrase "*More Lord*"? If that is the case, you are not alone.

When we encounter God, we become aware of his surpassing greatness, yet we are also aware of our limitations. How many stunning and profound stories have we read in the Bible and in church history about God's works? Anything is possible with God, and he works through imperfect people, yet why is it that we do not always see the more of God we desire?

As Christians, we can look for more of God in many places. This may be through studying and applying the Bible, an encounter with God during sung worship, an impartation of a spiritual gift, a daily habit of prayer and intercession, getting baptised and taking communion, or by being faithful with what God has entrusted to us.

If you want more of God, then you are in good company. When Jesus was washing his disciples' feet Peter initially objected, but

Jesus replied, "Unless I wash you, you have no part with me." (Jn. 13:8). Peter's response was "Then, Lord, not just my feet but my hands and my head as well!" (Jn. 13:9).

For Peter, having his feet washed by Jesus was not enough, he wanted more. Peter was 'all in', he was wholehearted, and he wanted more of what Jesus had to give him.[2] Yet despite his heart's desire for more, Peter misunderstood what Jesus was saying and why Jesus wanted to wash his feet.

Jesus did not compliment him for his words but said "Those who have had a bath need only to wash their feet; their whole body is clean. And you are clean." (Jn. 13:10). Peter misunderstood the importance of Jesus being a servant, not just to his disciples, but also to point to the greatest act of his servanthood – laying down his life for them and us.

We can also misunderstand what God requires of us to have more of him in our lives. Like Peter, Jesus may want to direct us in ways that we don't expect to experience more of God. If that is the case, will we respond as Peter did and say "No, you shall never wash my feet." (Jn. 13:8) or are we open to learning new lessons to receive more of God?

Through washing the disciples' feet, Jesus was not just teaching Peter the importance of being a servant, he was also teaching Peter the importance of doing what he did. Jesus was setting Peter an example, that he wanted him to put into practice (Jn. 13:15). Was Jesus saying to Peter, if you want more *of me* then you need to be more *like me*?

---

[2] Bible commentaries vary on their views of this passage with some agreeing Peter was wholehearted (e.g. Matthew Henry, Ellicots and Barnes). The majority agree that that the overriding context is one of Peter misunderstanding what Jesus was trying to teach his disciples about servanthood.

PREFACE

We can often use the phrase 'more of God', but the New Testament writers didn't use that terminology. The phrase that is closest to 'more of God' is the phrase 'fullness of God'. For example, the fullness of God is seen in Jesus and it is in Christ that we are brought to fullness.

> For in Christ all the fullness of the Deity lives in bodily form, and in Christ you have been brought to fullness.
>
> Colossians 2:9 & 10

Therefore, if we want to understand what the fullness of God looks like, we need to see what it looks like in Jesus' life. This is where the journey to more of God begins because Jesus is the only perfect and trustworthy example to us of what the fullness of God looks like in a person.

This is a crucial lesson for all of us. If we want more of God, then we need to put into practice what Jesus said and did. We need to live the same servant lifestyle that Jesus did. We need to discover what is important to Jesus and develop a lifestyle around *his* priorities. Our premise is that when we are faithful in doing this, we will experience the more of God.

The problem is that in our modern technological world, there is so much that demands our attention. There is so much clutter that can get in the way of following Jesus. Clutter can be defined as "to fill or cover with scattered or disordered things that impede movement or reduce effectiveness."[3]

It could be entertainment, fitness, social media, shopping, or work that gets in the way of following Jesus. Equally, it could be that our internal world is full of clutter. For many, their mental

---

[3] Merriam-Webster. https://www.merriam-webster.com/dictionary/clutter

wellbeing is under strain, which at times can sadly lead to unhealthy coping mechanisms.[4]

Our internal worlds are important to God because they include our thoughts, feelings, emotions, mindsets and belief systems. The more of God that we seek is linked to his power that is at work *within us*. It is when we are strengthened in our inner being and rooted in his love that we can be filled with all the fullness of God (Eph. 3:16-21).

Jesus came to set us free (Gal. 5:1). He came to set us free from sin, but also from the clutter that gets in the way of following him. This is Jesus' purpose for your life. He wants to set you free from external and internal clutter, so you are free and able to develop a lifestyle like his.

This is the way we can get more of God. Yet if we are being honest, many of us would want a simpler method. Many Christians and churches search for the quick-fix route to getting more of God in their lives. However much we seek more of God, if we don't follow the example that Jesus has given us, we are unlikely to obtain it.

Do you know a Christian who has become discouraged through an unfulfilled expectation they had of God or something that didn't happen? Hunger for more of God can get replaced by disappointment, discouragement and even rejection of faith. They knew there was more, but it somehow eluded them. Maybe they were looking for Jesus in the wrong places.

Yet how is it that some Christians do find more of God? Is it that they have realised the significance of the simple invitation

---

[4] Mighty Pursuit Team. "8 Eye-Opening Mental Health Statistics Around The Globe". *Mighty Pursuit.* https://mightypursuit.com/blog/8-eye-opening-mental-health-statistics-around-the-globe

from Jesus to follow him and replicate his lifestyle? Is it that they have learned to go to all the places where he is? After all, Jesus said, "Whoever serves me must follow me; and where I am, my servant also will be." (Jn. 12:26).

Can it be that more of God *is within our grasp*, but somehow, we have not found where Jesus is, and instead got caught up with our or other people's agendas and plans? Will we serve Jesus where he is rather than where we prefer to be? Finding Jesus is not an art or mystery because the Bible tells us where to find him.

Jesus's invitation to follow him is a daily practice and a lifelong endeavour. It is to join in with what he is already doing in Christians, churches, the unsaved and the marginalised. This is where we will find the more of God that we seek. The challenge is that Jesus wants us to go to *all the places* where he is and not pick and choose only the places we want to go to.

ACKNOWLEDGEMENTS

We would like to thank all those who have helped make this book possible. Whether from a theological, engagement, structural, insight or readability perspective, your advice has enriched this book.

We are particularly grateful to the following family and friends who have invested their time to make this book a reality: Corrine, David, Derrick, Esther, Janice, John, Joy, Julia, Liz, Mark, Nathan and Zoe.

We are grateful for your friendship over the years, especially during the difficult times in our lives. You have faithfully stood by and supported us in this and other ventures.

You are all an encouragement to us both. Our prayer for you all is that you will know the more of God.

ENDORSEMENTS

'We live in a world enslaved by the mantra of 'BIGGER-BETTER-FASTER-MORE'. This is observed in the microcosm of our daily quest for Bigger cloud storage, Better phone reception, Faster parcel delivery and More likes-shares-followers etc.

This book addresses the most pressing 'More' of human experience, 'How to encounter MORE of God?'. However, this is not some opaque treatise on the mysteries of Christian metaphysics. It is an intensely practical book that walks you through the obstacles preventing 'More', while gently confronting our self-prescribed solutions that often prolong the absence of encounter. Moving on, you are taken on a journey through the places where it is certain you will find 'More' of God.

Do not be misled by thinking 'this is just another Christian self-help guide'. Rather, it is a rich and reasoned journey into the heart of God. Skilfully laid out by those whose lives bear witness of the 'More' available to us all. Mark and Fiona's walk qualifies their talk and is what gives this work substance.

Mark Hendley, D.D. (h.c.) and Director of The Stones Cry Out

If you are looking to recalibrate your understanding of discipleship, if you are longing to know and truly experience more of God and who you are in Him, if you want to understand a fruitful life from Heaven's perspective, this book is for you. It doesn't just offer excellent information; it provides a roadmap for you to experience a transformation.

In the 7+ years I have known Mark & Fiona, they have consistently impressed me with their wanting more of God, their courage in obeying His words, and the working out of their faith in action. "*It may be time for a reality check as to what is most important to us and whether we are following Jesus casually or wholeheartedly.*" I have witnessed them live out the teaching in these pages, even in the most challenging of times.

I admire them for sharing such personal vulnerability in this powerful presentation of how "*true discipleship is to spend time with Jesus so that we become like him and do what he does (Jn. 8:31-32)*".

Janice Pleasants, Leads Online Eastgate School of Spiritual Life

This inspiring book combines excellent insights from Scripture with brilliant engagement of today's Western culture, on how to be filled with God's glory and pass it on to others. It's a must read for the thirsty!

Derrick Burns, Author, Speaker & Founder of Ministry School Intl.

If you want a down to earth, practical, wisdom-filled book on how to "attain to the fullness of Christ", then this is the one for you.

Mark and Fiona have used their wealth of experience and examples of their own journeys in pursuing more of Jesus, which adds reality and grounding to the pages.

Dave Smith, Leader, River of Life Church, Eastbourne
Co-ordinator, Langney Shopping Centre Chaplaincy Team

The Son is the image of the invisible God, the firstborn over all creation. For in him all things were created: things in heaven and on earth, visible and invisible, whether thrones or powers or rulers or authorities; all things have been created through him and for him.

He is before all things, and in him all things hold together. And he is the head of the body, the church; he is the beginning and the firstborn from among the dead, so that in everything he might have the supremacy.

For God was pleased to have all his fullness dwell in him, and through him to reconcile to himself all things, whether things on earth or things in heaven, by making peace through his blood, shed on the cross.

The apostle Paul, speaking of Jesus Christ
(Colossians 1:15-20)

PART ONE
REMOVING CLUTTER

We make space, we make room. How we long to be close to You.

Oh come and take up residence. Jesus, Jesus, welcome in.

We're clearing out the clutter. For the only One that matters.

We're clearing out the clutter. You're the only One we're after.

We make space, we make space. Space, there's space for You.

We Make Space, Melissa Helser

MAKING SPACE FOR JESUS

We must let go of the life we have planned, so as to accept the one that is waiting for us.
(Joseph Campbell, Writer)

Sort Your Life Out

The BBC television show Sort Your Life Out is very popular in the UK and was dubbed "perfect television" by a national newspaper.[5] Within the show, a team helps families declutter their houses, which are often this way for lots of reasons, including holding onto items for emotional reasons. Families have to sift through their possessions so that at least half can be sold, recycled or donated to charity.

The way this is done is to completely empty their house and lay out all their possessions in a warehouse. They then have two days to sort through all their clutter whilst inevitably dealing with emotions that are linked to specific items. The items could be related to a past event or a family member who is unwell or has died.

Whilst this is happening, the team redecorates, alters, upcycles and cleans their home to improve the living areas and to make space for only the possessions they need. Once the home is finished and the items are organised within it, the family then

---

[5] Golby, Joel. "Sort Your Life Out With Stacey Solomon: this is perfect TV – and I don't say that lightly". *The Guardian*. https://www.theguardian.com/tv-and-radio/2021/nov/04/sort-your-life-out-with-stacey-solomon-this-is-perfect-tv-and-i-dont-say-that-lightly

returns and is united with their home, often with overflowing tears and thanks.

Three months later the family is visited to see how their lives have improved since the house makeover. In the majority of cases, now that the external and internal clutter has been removed, families have stronger relationships, are happier and can function well. Such is the impact of removing clutter we do not need!

"Why are you striving? God doesn't want you to strive."

It is 1994 and I (Mark) am in a church meeting experiencing the tangible presence of God in a way I have not done before. I am looking around at my friends encountering God – some are laughing and some are crying, yet it does not seem to bother any of them. I am surprised at what I see because I was not expecting this.

In previous years I read about Christian revivals throughout history and God had developed a hunger in me to experience more of him. As an evangelist, I have in this moment a fresh desire to see many more people become Christians. I start to think, is this the beginning of a revival, will this satisfy my hunger for Jesus?

One of the leaders in the church that I was visiting came over to me and asked if they could pray for me, which I accepted. In my mind, I was thinking I wanted a baptism of fire and power, so I could become more effective at sharing my faith with unbelievers. The church leader then said to me, "Why are you striving? God doesn't want you to strive."

I thought, what has that got to do with revival? Then I suddenly became aware of how much my Christian life was based on striving, that I was working out of my own strength rather than allowing God to work in and through me. I also realised that I was working hard to please God to gain his approval. I started to wonder if God loved and delighted in me just as I was.

Over the next few years, I had many profound love encounters with Father God as he rewired my thinking, my sense of self-worth and my identity. I was also not alone; thousands of Christians across the globe encountered Father God in similar ways. I began to understand what it meant to be *a child* of God.

Looking back, I realise that I had clutter in my life (like striving) that was stopping me from experiencing God in his fullness. I didn't need to be perfect (phew!), but I did need to make some changes in my life if I wanted more of God. It mattered what I thought and believed about myself, others, and God. It also mattered whether I would make it a priority to pursue him and increasingly see things from his perspective.

Making space for God

IKEA, the multinational conglomerate, is known for its interior design being associated with simplicity. Its advertising campaigns over the years have included phrases like "Escape the clutter", "Goodbye messy. Hello neat!", and "Make Room For Your Life". IKEA claims that clutter is among the most common causes of fights in the home.

The amazing truth is that God wants to make his home in us. The writer of Hebrews says, "For every house is built by someone, but God is the builder of everything... But Christ is faithful as the Son over God's house. And we are his house, if indeed we hold firmly to our confidence and the hope in which we glory" (Heb. 3:4 & 6).

Part of the process of God making his home in us is to make room in our lives for what is most important to him. The same is true with other important relationships we make. If we start dating someone then we make space for them in our lives. If a new child or grandchild comes into the family, we make space to welcome and care for them.

A relationship is healthy if those within it seek to understand what is important to the other in it. If they don't, then their relationship is unlikely to function well. Making space for those that we love shows how much they mean to us. Yet even in a healthy relationship, there can be times when clutter can get in the way.

When this occurs, the clutter can take up the space that would be naturally given to those we love, including God. Any clutter in our lives that gets in the way of us experiencing more of God's fullness is something that he will want to clear out. To pursue God means that we need to make more space for him in our lives.

Why is that? It is because clutter gets in the way of God achieving all that he plans in and through us. Clutter can be defined as "a lot of things in an untidy state, especially things that are not useful or necessary" and "to run in disorder; move with bustle and confusion."[6] The more space God gets in our lives, the more profound his works through us can be.

In the last week of Jesus' life, he fulfilled a messianic prophecy by entering Jerusalem on a donkey (Zech. 9:9). When he arrives at the temple, what is the first thing he does? He makes a whip and drives out the money changers and those selling cattle,

---

[6] Collins. https://www.collinsdictionary.com/dictionary/english/clutter; *Dictionary.com*.https://www.dictionary.com/browse/clutter

sheep and doves (Jn. 2:13-25). Tables are turned over and coins are scattered.

We know historically that Jesus' actions were in reaction to the Temple establishment being corrupt. The Jewish ruling aristocracy at the time was making significant profits from taxes and selling animals for sacrifice.[7] Jesus' rebuke was, "To those who sold doves he said, 'Get these out of here! Stop turning my Father's house into a market!'" (Jn. 2:16).

Was Jesus only concerned with the corruption of the temple? Jesus would have cared about how the Temple establishment co-operated with the aristocracy in the exploitation of the poor, but his rebuke focused on the function of his Father's house, i.e. it should not be a market.

In Matthew's gospel, Jesus' rebuke is "My house will be called a house of prayer, but you are making it 'a den of robbers.'" (Mt. 21:13). Here Jesus is combining two Old Testament verses from Isaiah 56:7 and Jeremiah 7:11, both of which would have been understood by his Jewish audience.

In the Jewish education system, children learn the Torah by heart.[8] This committed-to-mind knowledge allows for a very specific way of rabbinic teaching. When Jesus (or any other rabbi) quotes a single verse from a passage, the audience understands the rabbi is referring to the whole passage, not just the verse.

Isaiah's prophecy speaks about the joy God will give to both Jews and Gentiles who hold fast to the covenant and keep the

---

[7] Nappa, Mike. "Who Were the Sadducees in the Bible? What Were Their Beliefs?" *Christianity.com*. https://www.christianity.com/wiki/people/who-were-the-sadducees-in-the-bible-what-were-their-beliefs.html

[8] Talor, Joan. *Boy Jesus: Growing Up Judaean in Turbulent Times*. SPCK Publishing, 2025. See also Deuteronomy 11:18-21.

Sabbath. Their prayers will be accepted, and his house will be called "a house of prayer for all nations" (Isa. 56:7). The prophecy also speaks about how Israel's watchmen are blind, lack understanding and have unhealthy appetites – this would have been a stinging rebuke for the Jewish leaders.

Jeremiah's prophecy is a call for reformation so that God will continue to let them live in Jerusalem. He said, "if you do not oppress the foreigner, the fatherless or the widow and do not shed innocent blood in this place, and if you do not follow other gods to your own harm, then I will let you live in this place." (Jer. 7:6-7). Sadly, they did not respond to Jeremiah's prophecy or Jesus' rebuke and the Temple was destroyed in CE 70.[9]

The Temple was a large building complex which featured several dedicated sections, one of which was The Court of the Gentiles.[10] This place was reserved so that Gentiles (non-Jews) could come and worship the God of Israel. The market had been set up in this court which prevented Gentiles from having a place to come to worship and pray.

The clutter that Jesus is clearing out of the Temple focuses on corruption and unfaithfulness but it also includes clearing out anything that stops the marginalised (i.e. foreigner, the fatherless and widows) and the Gentiles from coming to him. Within the context of this story, the equivalent of the Gentiles for us as Christians would be those who are unsaved.

What are Jesus' priorities here? Yes, he wants us to have clean lives, be faithful to his words, and worship him. But he also wants us to make space in our lives for the foreigner, the

---

[9] Weksler-Bdolah, Shlomit. Aelia *Capitolina* - Jerusalem in the Roman period: In light of archaeological research. BRILL, 2019.
[10] Schiffman, Lawrence H. *Understanding Second Temple and Rabbinic Judaism*. Ktav Pub & Distributors Inc, 2003.

fatherless, the widow and the unsaved. God does not want any clutter in our lives that hinders people who don't know him, from coming to him.

After Jesus cleared the temple courts, there was space for the blind and lame to come to him and be healed, which led to children spontaneously shouting praise to God! (Mt. 21:14-16). If we want to see God miraculously heal people through us, it may be that we first need to clear out some clutter and make space in our lives for his priorities.

What happened at the Temple that day can be seen as a blueprint for our lives with God. If we make space for God in our lives then we can know his fullness. Jesus says, "Blessed are those who hunger and thirst for righteousness, for they will be filled." (Mt. 5:6). If we declutter our lives and hunger and thirst for his kingdom, we will be filled with him.

What does the fullness of God look like in our lives?

The fullness of God is mentioned several times within the New Testament, primarily in Ephesians and Colossians. Fullness encompasses to be filled, to make full, to abound, full measure, to make complete, to bring to realisation, to accomplish, to make perfect, and fullness of time.[11]

The fullness of God is far more than an experience or feeling – it describes a lifestyle that is full of God. The apostle Paul, speaking of Jesus, says "For God was pleased to have all his fullness dwell in him" (Col. 1:19). If we want to see what the fullness of God looks like in a person's life, we need to see what it looked like in Jesus' life.

---

[11] plēroō, Strong's G4137; plērōma, Strong's G4138

This is important because Jesus' life was not an easy, problem-free life. Yes, there were miracles, salvation, and angelic encounters, but there were also persecution and suffering. Pursuing the fullness of God will come at a price. To truly know the fullness of God we need to model our lives on Jesus, having the same priorities that he did, and spending time doing the things he did.

More than that, we need to seek to emulate Jesus' relationship with Father God. Jesus said to his disciple Philip:

> Anyone who has seen me has seen the Father. How can you say, "Show us the Father"? Don't you believe that I am in the Father, and that the Father is in me? The words I say to you I do not speak on my own authority. Rather, it is the Father, living in me, who is doing his work.
>
> John 14:9-10

If we have the fullness of God in our lives it will reveal Jesus, his nature, his love, and his kindness. When people meet us, we hope they will encounter Jesus. This is a measure we can use to see if we are growing in the fullness of God. As God does his work in us, it will affect our character, but it will also impact people around us.

Paul prays an amazing prayer for the Christians in Ephesus:

> I pray that out of his glorious riches he may strengthen you with power through his Spirit in your inner being, so that Christ may dwell in your hearts through faith. And I pray that you, being rooted and established in love, may have power, together with all the Lord's holy people, to grasp how wide and long and high and deep

is the love of Christ, and to know this love that surpasses knowledge – that you may be filled to the measure of all the fullness of God.

> Ephesians 3:16-19

This helps us in our understanding of how to live in the fullness of God. Paul describes four key aspects. Firstly, Christ may dwell in our hearts. If we want to model our lives on Jesus, what better way is there to achieve this than having Christ dwell inside of us? As we make room for him in our lives, we will begin to think, feel and prioritise like he does.

Secondly, we are rooted and established in love. God is love (1 Jn. 4:16). Knowing about God's love is different to *knowing* God's love. To truly know God's love means we are fully aware and conscious of the fact that we and others are loved. Knowing God's love affects our identity, self-worth, and our value of other people.

Thirdly, we grasp the vastness of God's love. God's love is not small or limited, it is not a fleeting emotion, it defines who God is. It should also define who we are. Not only personally, but collectively, because Paul says, it requires all of God's people to comprehend how vast God's love is (Eph. 3:18-19).

Fourthly, we may be filled with the fullness of God. This was Paul's desire, he was not praying for a temporary or half-filling, rather he prayed they would experience *all* the fullness of God. We would suggest Paul prayed this because the church would then fully represent what the Father is like, so that the world may know who the church belongs to (Jn. 13:34-35).

Are you ready for a journey?

For both of us, our twenties were very formative. We experienced profound love encounters with God and they established in us a belief that God had more for us; all we needed to do was to go and find it. Over the decades that followed, we went after more, travelling to several countries and churches in our desire to know him more. We had some life-changing adventures.

Yet there was still more to learn. You can't press a button and get all of God in a moment. God does not seem to be in a rush. God seems content to bring us his fullness through both the profound and ordinary moments of life. There is also more of God to be experienced in the difficult moments of life such as disappointment, discouragement and even suffering.

At times in our lives, it was within reach and other times it seemed to elude us. There were times when we had momentum and other times we got stuck and wanted to give up. Yet we found God to always be faithful and to always have answers, even when we couldn't see the way forward.

We don't get all the fullness of God the moment we are born again. Oh, if it were that simple! It requires a journey where we continually follow Jesus throughout our life, so he can transform us into his likeness (2 Cor. 3:18). It takes time for us to understand who Jesus is and what is important to him.

When we are born again, we are set free from sin (Rom. 6:18) and given the nature of God (2 Pet. 1:4). As we put Jesus' words into practice and renew our minds (Rom. 12:2), we start to build a strong foundation for our lives (Mt. 7:24-27). This foundation is built upon how Jesus, the Word made flesh, thinks, speaks and acts (Jn. 1:14).

As our foundation is established, we can live in more of the fullness of God. Paul speaks about the importance of Christians being equipped and built up in love "until we all reach unity in the faith and in the knowledge of the Son of God and become mature, attaining to the whole measure of the fullness of Christ." (Eph. 4:13). It is a journey centred on God's love that we can all do together.

The apostle Peter describes the journey like this:

> Make every effort to add to your faith goodness; and to goodness, knowledge; and to knowledge, self-control; and to self-control, perseverance; and to perseverance, godliness; and to godliness, mutual affection; and to mutual affection, love.
>
> For if you possess these qualities in increasing measure, they will keep you from being ineffective and unproductive in your knowledge of our Lord Jesus Christ.
>
> Peter 1:5-8

Peter says we are meant to add to our initial faith knowledge, perseverance, and mutual affection, arriving at love. This is the journey we all need to go on so that we can be filled with the full measure of God. Do you want to go further? Maybe you have got stuck? Is it something you are truly prepared to give time and effort to?

God has led us to experience more of his fullness, but not always in the way we expected. We are also still a work in progress, we are still learning and growing. God is still leading us and we are still challenged to keep following him. Our story includes personal growth and miracles, but also how we have struggled with disappointment and trauma.

We hope that our stories will help you on your journey to know God in his fullness. Whether you are experiencing his favour and thriving or whether God seems to be distant, and you are struggling, this book will help with both, because both are part of the journey to know his fullness.

Each of the chapters within this book includes a reflection. These are designed to connect you with Father God so he can take you step-by-step along this journey. We want you to primarily be led by him, rather than following a method. We would encourage you to take time to go through the reflections.

Within each reflection, take time to talk and listen to God. We encourage you to write down what you hear. Then make time to pray about and meditate on what God has said to you. If you did not hear anything, ask Father God to help you hear his voice and listen again. Finally, put into practice what you have heard and read, as that is how we grow.

Will you make space in your life for more of Jesus?

Reflection

Consider these verses:

> *And foreigners who bind themselves to the Lord to minister to him, to love the name of the Lord, and to be his servants, all who keep the Sabbath without desecrating it and who hold fast to my covenant— these I will bring to my holy mountain and give them joy in my house of prayer. Their burnt offerings and sacrifices will be accepted on my altar; for my house will be called a house of prayer for all nations.*
>
> Isaiah 56:6-7

Ask Father God:

- Lord, what foundations have you already put in my life that enable me to know your fullness?
- Lord, what does it look like for you to make your home within my life?
- Lord, what is my next step on the journey to being more like Jesus?

Prayer:

> *Thank you that you love me and your plans for me are good. Please show me how I can make more room for you in my life. Please show me what clutter is in the way. Help me understand what your priorities are and how I can create a lifestyle that aligns with them.*

To do:

- Make a list of any clutter that you may have in your life.
- Pray through the list and ask Father God to help you remove the clutter.

Further reading:

- Ephesians 3:14-21
- 2 Peter 1:3-10
- 2 Corinthians 5:16-21

DO NOT WORRY

Worry does not empty tomorrow of its sorrow, it empties today of its strength.
(Corrie Ten Boom, Author & Speaker)

"When did you last feel safe?"

I (Mark) was part of a ministry team that was praying for people to be healed at a weekend conference. During the meeting, I felt I should go to the back of the hall. As I got near the back I saw a young woman shaking with fear. Standing next to and supporting the young woman was her Grandma. I went over to them and introduced myself.

Grandma explained that this young woman had experienced trauma and since then had struggled with significant anxiety. I asked the young woman if I could pray for her and she agreed. I asked Jesus to bring his peace to her life and remove the impact of the trauma. After praying, the Holy Spirit gave me a question to ask the young woman.

I asked her "When did you last feel safe?". She replied, "When I was a young child sitting on my Dad's knee." I then asked, "What was your Dad doing to make you feel safe?" She replied, "He was stroking my hair behind my ear." I didn't know what to do next but prayed for her some more.

I asked a female team member to come and help and decided to go and pray for some other people. Later I came back to see how the young woman was doing. The Grandma greeted me excitedly! She told me that after I had left, her Dad had come over to see his daughter. The Grandma then explained to him the question I had asked his daughter.

The young woman's Dad then started to stroke his daughter's hair behind her ear as the female team member prayed for her. She immediately started to relax and powerfully encountered the love of God. It was as though before this moment, anxiety was making it difficult for her to receive from God.

The Grandma then shared with me more about her backstory. It was sad to hear and the reasons for her anxiety were clear. She had rarely left her house for nearly a year and coming to this meeting was a significantly brave thing to do. That is why she was shaking with anxiety and was standing at the back.

The good news was that the young woman decided to go back to her parent's house after the meeting to share a meal with them. She had not felt able to do this for many months, which was a sign that God had touched her deeply. I was struck by how intimately and beautifully God knows each one of us and how he can reach us when we feel far from him.

The scale of mental health problems

As a Western society, it seems in some ways we are only really starting to understand mental health and its impact on people's lives. The majority of government and private health care is still spent on physical health. In 2022/23, the NHS in the UK spent

14% of its budget on mental health, which was an increase of 13.8% in 2021/22.[12]

It is estimated that more than 84 million people in Europe are struggling with mental health issues, which equates to 19% of the population.[13] In 2021, 22.8% of U.S. adults (57.8 million) experienced a mental health illness.[14] During the COVID-19 pandemic, anxiety disorders grew worldwide from about 298 million to 374 million people affected.[15]

Mental health conditions are still not widely understood in Western society and are therefore often hidden or suppressed. In the UK, mental health problems now account for the majority of days lost due to work-related ill health.[16] Even though mental health issues affect so many, there is still a great deal of stigma around them.

In response to this, employers, health organisations and charities have introduced articles, courses, treatments and support groups. The language of mindfulness is becoming more common and self-help book sales have grown 30% in 2022.[17] In 2019 Barnes & Noble bookstores saw mental health books outsell diet and exercise books.[18]

---

[12] NHS England. "Mental health services funding and investment". *NHS England.* https://www.england.nhs.uk/mental-health/taskforce/imp/mh-dashboard.
[13] Amand-Eeckhout, Laurence. "Mental health in the EU", *European Parliament.* https://www.europarl.europa.eu/RegData/etudes/BRIE/2023/751416/EPRS_BRI(2023)751416_EN.pdf
[14] NAMI. "Mental Health By the Numbers". *National Alliance on Mental Illness.* https://nami.org/mhstats
[15] Duszynski-Goodman, Lizzie. "Mental Health Statistics And Facts". *Forbes.* https://www.forbes.com/health/mind/mental-health-statistics
[16] HSE. "Working days lost in Great Britain". *Health and Safety Executive.* https://www.hse.gov.uk/statistics/dayslost.htm
[17] Curcic, Dimitrije. "Self-Help Books Statistics". *WordsRated.* https://wordsrated.com/self-help-books-statistics
[18] Schaub, Michael. "Mental health books outsell diet and exercise books at Barnes & Noble". *Los Angeles Times.* https://www.latimes.com/books/la-et-jc-mental-heath-book-sales-20190111-story.html

The good news is that most people can recover partially or fully from mental health problems.[19] Despite this, the main challenge remains the wait time to access mental health services. In the UK, research suggests nearly one in four are being forced to wait more than 12 weeks to start treatment.[20]

Those living in poverty see an increased risk of mental health, for both adults and children. The U.S. National Library of Medicine states "Despite their high need for mental health services, children and families living in poverty are least likely to be connected with high-quality mental health care".[21]

The impact of war significantly continues to impact people's mental health. Care International reported that an estimated one-third of Ukrainian refugees are expected to develop depression, anxiety, or post-traumatic stress disorder.[22] A survey by the Refugee Council in England found that 61% of asylum seekers experience serious mental illness.[23]

It is estimated more people die globally from mental health problems each year than have died globally from COVID-19.[24] These estimates suggest mental health problems are one of the

---

[19] Neuroscience News. "Study Finds That People Can Recover and Thrive After Mental Illness and Substance-Use Disorders". *Neuroscience News*. http://neurosciencenews.com/thriving-mental-health-20323; NHS England. "NHS welcomes record high recovery rate for common mental illness". *NHS England*. https://www.england.nhs.uk/2018/02/mental-illness-recovery

[20] NHS England. "Mental health access and waiting time standards". *NHS England*. https://www.england.nhs.uk/mental-health/resources/access-waiting-time

[21] Hodgkinson, Stacy (PhD). "Improving Mental Health Access for Low-Income Children and Families in the Primary Care Setting". *NCBI*. https://www.ncbi.nlm.nih.gov/pmc/articles/PMC5192088

[22] CARE International. "Six months on in Ukraine: Brutal mental health toll must not be overlooked, warns CARE". *Care*. https://www.care-international.org/news/six-months-ukraine-brutal-mental-health-toll-must-not-be-overlooked-warns-care

[23] House of Commons Library. "Refugee mental health and the response to the humanitarian crisis in Ukraine". *UK Parliament*. https://commonslibrary.parliament.uk/refugee-mental-health-and-the-response-to-the-humanitarian-crisis-in-ukraine

[24] Reisinger Walker, Elizabeth. "Mortality in Mental Disorders and Global Disease Burden Implications". *NCBI*. https://www.ncbi.nlm.nih.gov/pmc/articles/PMC4461039; World Health Organisation. "Number of COVID-19 cases reported to WHO". *World Health Organisation*. https://covid19.who.int/

highest causes of death worldwide. Poor or deteriorating mental health has become one of the greatest 'pandemics' of the modern world.

The scale of this issue raises some big questions for us as Christians. Do we believe God has solutions for mental health problems? Do we believe that God can restore mental ill-health? Do we believe what the Bible says about the mind? What does Jesus have to say about mental health?

Understanding Worry and Anxiety

Worry is defined as feeling "unhappy and frightened because of problems or unpleasant things that might happen."[25] Anxiety is defined as "an uncomfortable feeling of nervousness or worry about something that is happening or might happen in the future."[26] Worry tends to be temporary whereas anxiety can linger.[27]

Worrying is feeling uneasy or being overly concerned about a situation or problem. It is not always a negative thing. It can "improve your attention and problem-solving, motivate you to work harder toward a goal, or warn you about a potential threat". For example, you may worry about money, health and relationships.

Anxiety is the reaction to situations that you perceive as stressful or dangerous. Anxiety tends to overestimate the risk of such situations and can be hard to manage. It can also affect our ability to function and can impair daily living activities. Severe

---

[25] Cambridge Dictionary. https://dictionary.cambridge.org/dictionary/english/worry
[26] Cambridge Dictionary. https://dictionary.cambridge.org/dictionary/english/anxiety
[27] Henry Ford Health Staff. "Worry and Anxiety: Do You Know the Difference?". *Henry Ford Health.* https://www.henryford.com/blog/2020/08/the-difference-between-worry-and-anxiety

levels of anxiety are a mental health condition which requires treatment to resolve.

There are several anxiety disorders, here are the most commonly diagnosed according to the organisation MIND:

- **Generalised anxiety disorder (GAD)** – this means having regular or uncontrollable worries about many different things in your everyday life.
- **Social anxiety disorder** – this diagnosis means you experience extreme fear or anxiety triggered by social situations (such as parties, workplaces, or everyday situations where you have to talk to another person).
- **Panic disorder** – this means having regular or frequent panic attacks without a clear cause or trigger. Experiencing panic disorder can mean that you feel constantly afraid of having another panic attack, to the point that this fear itself can trigger your panic attacks.
- **Phobias** – a phobia is an extreme fear or anxiety triggered by a particular situation (such as going outside) or a particular object (such as spiders).
- **Post-traumatic stress disorder (PTSD)** – this is a diagnosis you may be given if you develop anxiety problems after going through something you found traumatic. PTSD can involve experiencing flashbacks or nightmares which can feel like you're re-living all the fear and anxiety you experienced at the time of the traumatic events.
- **Obsessive-compulsive disorder (OCD)** – you may be given this diagnosis if your anxiety problems involve having repetitive thoughts, behaviours or urges you can't control.
- **Health anxiety** – this means you experience obsessions and compulsions relating to illness, including

researching symptoms or checking to see if you have them.
- **Body dysmorphic disorder (BDD)** – this means you experience obsessions and compulsions relating to your physical appearance.
- **Perinatal anxiety or perinatal OCD** – some people develop anxiety problems during pregnancy or in the first year after giving birth.[28]

The effects of anxiety can be felt in both our mind and body. In the mind, these can include a sense of dread, an inability to stop worrying, low mood, depersonalisation and rumination. In the body, these can include a churning feeling in the stomach, dizziness, headaches, restlessness, fast breathing and sleep problems.

The main causes of anxiety are traumatic experiences, stress, illegal drugs, the side effects of medication, serious health problems, learnt behaviour and brain chemistry. Worry and anxiety are internal clutter that we don't want in our lives. It is not something that we should accept as normal. Help can be found through relevant therapy, support, and prayer.

It is likely there will often be circumstances around us that cause us to worry or be afraid. Fear, anxiety and worry can rob us of so much. It can stop us from living in the fullness of God, pursuing our dreams, following God's plan for our lives and enjoying a healthy life and relationships.

When we worry or are anxious; we can continually rehearse a problem or situation in our mind, which can become mentally and physically draining. Our emotions and thoughts can

---

[28] Mind. "Anxiety and panic attacks". *Mind.* https://www.mind.org.uk/information-support/types-of-mental-health-problems/anxiety-and-panic-attacks/anxiety-disorders

become consumed with our concerns and fears. This can lead to a sense of powerlessness and a belief that there is nothing we can do about the problem or situation.

Contrast this with what a healthy internal world looks like for a Christian. A healthy mind meditates on the goodness and strength of God, knowing that he is trustworthy and present in all situations, and knowing "God is our refuge and strength, an ever-present help in trouble". (Ps. 46:1).

Jesus understands what it is like to suffer anxiety. In the garden of Gethsemane, he was anticipating his crucifixion and he was in deep anguish. He prayed "Father, if you are willing, take this cup from me; yet not my will, but yours be done." (Lk. 22:42). Jesus knew what was ahead – being subjected to excruciating pain, devasting humiliation, and an agonising death.[29]

During his prayer, an angel appeared to him to strengthen him and his sweat was like drops of blood falling to the ground (Lk. 22:43-44.). Under conditions of extreme stress and anxiety, a human can sweat blood. Research shows this can happen in people awaiting execution.[30]

In Hebrews it says of Jesus that "we do not have a high priest who is unable to feel sympathy for our weaknesses, but we have one who has been tempted in every way, just as we are – yet he did not sin." (Heb. 4:15). Jesus has compassion for us when we feel weak and overwhelmed.

This includes when we worry and are anxious because Jesus can relate to such moments. We therefore don't need to feel we

---

[29] Crucifixion was a brutal form of capital punishment, it was purposely designed to achieve a prolonged, agonising death.
[30] Jerajani, H. R. "Hematohidrosis – A Rare Clinical Phenomenon". *NCBI.* https://www.ncbi.nlm.nih.gov/pmc/articles/PMC2810702

are somehow out of touch with or far from Father God when we suffer anxiety. One of the messianic prophecies says Jesus would be "despised and rejected by mankind, a man of suffering, and familiar with pain." (Isa. 53:3).

There is no shame if we are struggling with worry or experiencing anxiety. The cross was considered a shameful way to die, yet though Jesus endured it, he scorned its shame (Heb. 12:2).[31] Jesus wants to help us so that we can throw off everything that hinders us and run the race God has marked out for us (Heb. 12:1).

We can feel shame because we may be embarrassed to ask for help, don't know how to find a solution or think we deserve to struggle due to our own poor choices. It may occur if we struggle with anxiety. The answer to shame is not to judge ourselves or others but rather to show empathy and kindness to ourselves and others.

What does the Bible say about anxiety and worry?

Firstly, it is important to know who we belong to – God is our place of safety. David declares that God has "been my refuge and a strong tower against the foe" (Ps. 61:3). He declares this when his "heart grows faint" (Ps. 61:2) when he is on the run for his life from his son Absalom (2 Sam. 15:13-37).[32]

In these dire circumstances, David is reminding himself who he belongs to and that God is his place of safety (Prv. 18:10). Knowing who God is and being in a place of safety are key to overcoming worry and anxiety. We are seated with Christ in

---

[31] Retief, F. P. "The history and pathology of crucifixion". *NCBI.* https://pubmed.ncbi.nlm.nih.gov/14750495

[32] This is the view of most scholars.

heavenly places and so our soul is eternally safe, regardless of our earthly circumstances (Eph. 2:6).

We can feel safe because we belong to God. This sense of safety can pervade our bodies and minds. Whatever support, prayer, encouragement, counselling and therapy we may receive to help us overcome worry and anxiety, God's love and care need to be our foundation. When our feelings overwhelm us, we can, like David, declare that God is our refuge.

Secondly, we need to know and experience God's love for us. It is not just knowing logically that he loves us, but we experience his love being "poured out into our hearts through the Holy Spirit". (Rom. 5:5). Poured in this passage has a sense of gushing and streams – it is not a trickle! [33]

The apostle John says:

> If anyone acknowledges that Jesus is the Son of God, God lives in them and they in God. And so we know and rely on the love God has for us.
>
> God is love. Whoever lives in love lives in God, and God in them. This is how love is made complete among us so that we will have confidence on the day of judgment: in this world we are like Jesus.
>
> There is no fear in love. But perfect love drives out fear, because fear has to do with punishment. The one who fears is not made perfect in love.
>
> 1 John 4:15-18

---

[33] ekcheō, Strong's G1632

If we still fear, then one reason for that may be that we have not yet been made perfect in love. God's love has the power to drive out fear and keep it at bay. Love is infinitely more powerful than fear, anxiety and worry. The Holy Spirit inside of us means we are not timid or fearful and that we have love, power, a sound mind and self-discipline (2 Tim. 1:7).

Thirdly, knowing who God has made us – we are adopted as his children. The apostle Paul tells us "the Spirit you received brought about your adoption to sonship. And by him we cry, 'Abba, Father.'" (Rom. 8:15). Adoption to sonship here is a term referring to the full legal standing and benefits of an adopted male heir in Roman culture.[34]

Being a child of God means we no longer need to live in fear (Rom. 8:15). Fear is not part of our identity as a child of God, rather being assured of God's great love for us, is. This is not just a concept for our minds to understand, it is also something to experience in our emotions. We are invited to grasp how high, wide, long and deep is the love of Christ (Eph. 3:18).

We can experience God's love in our inmost being – heart, mind, soul and spirit, which can result in fear being driven out. This is not something to simply acknowledge, rather it is something to seek, experience, wonder at and learn to dwell in. When we experience his love we can feel safe. We don't have to live with worry and anxiety.

Fourthly, Jesus is the king of a new kingdom that we are part of. The gospel is about Jesus' kingship. The gospel of the kingdom was Jesus' mandate as a new anointed king (Mt. 24:14). The term 'gospel' means good news, but in the context of a new

---

[34] Scripture Union. "Sons and Heirs". *Scripture Union USA.*
https://scriptureunion.org/dailydiscovery/sons-and-heirs

triumphant king, the term 'gospel' is referred to as the royal announcement about a new king.[35]

So when Jesus says the following in the synagogue at Nazareth, he is describing what his kingship looks like:

> 'The Spirit of the Lord is on me, because he has anointed me to proclaim good news to the poor.
>
> He has sent me to proclaim freedom for the prisoners and recovery of sight for the blind,
> to set the oppressed free, to proclaim the year of the Lord's favour.'
>
> Then he rolled up the scroll, gave it back to the attendant and sat down. The eyes of everyone in the synagogue were fastened on him. He began by saying to them, 'Today this scripture is fulfilled in your hearing.'
>
> Luke 4:18-21

Jesus is drawing on the Messianic prophecies in Isaiah 58 and 61, so his Jewish audience knew the full context of what he was communicating. In these chapters, Jesus makes it clear that his kingdom will include setting captives free, comforting those who mourn, a crown of beauty instead of ashes, oil instead of mourning and praise instead of despair.

For those of us who have suffered anxiety, how often have we mourned, felt despair and sat in emotional ashes? If that is you, King Jesus has the answers in his kingdom to give to you. He offers a lifestyle in relationship with him that overcomes all of

---

[35] Bible Project. "Gospel of the Kingdom". *Bible Project.* https://bibleproject.com/videos/gospel-kingdom

these (Rom. 8:37). He offers us "righteousness, peace and joy in the Holy Spirit" (Rom. 14:17).

Fifthly, we can live in peace – a peaceful body and mind can be our norm. The Hebrew word šālôm means peace, harmony, wholeness, completeness, prosperity, health, safety, welfare, friendship and tranquillity.[36] Biblically, shalom is seen in reference to the wellbeing of others.[37]

The Hebrew word for shalom is שָׁלוֹם and in Jewish thinking these characters can be read from right to left. Each of these characters can have a meaning because they correspond to other Hebrew words. When they are placed together the meaning is that peace comes when you destroy (Sheen) the authority (Lamed) that causes (Vav) chaos (Mem).[38]

Theologian Cornelius Plantinga describes the biblical concept of shalom:

> The webbing together of God, humans, and all creation in justice, fulfilment, and delight is what the Hebrew prophets call shalom. We call it peace but it means far more than mere peace of mind or a cease-fire between enemies.
>
> In the Bible, shalom means universal flourishing, wholeness and delight – a rich state of affairs in which natural needs are satisfied and natural gifts fruitfully employed, a state of affairs that inspires joyful wonder as its Creator and Saviour opens doors and welcomes the creatures in whom he

---

[36] Strong's H7965
[37] Soroski, Jason. "What Does Shalom Mean & Why Is it Important?". *Crosswalk.com.* https://www.crosswalk.com/faith/spiritual-life/what-does-shalom-mean.html
[38] Discipleship Development. "Peace comes when you destroy the authority that causes chaos". *Discipleship Development.* https://developdisciples.files.wordpress.com/2020/07/shalom-definition.pdf

delights. Shalom, in other words, is the way things ought to be. [39]

This is not just a concept because it can be a practical reality. The apostle Peter encourages us to:

> Cast all your anxiety on him because he cares for you.
>
> 1 Peter 5:7

> Do not be anxious about anything, but in every situation, by prayer and petition, with thanksgiving, present your requests to God. And the peace of God, which transcends all understanding, will guard your hearts and your minds in Christ Jesus.
>
> Philippians 4:6-7

When we enter Jesus' kingdom we can experience shalom, because he says to us:

> Peace I leave with you; my peace I give you. I do not give to you as the world gives.
>
> Do not let your hearts be troubled and do not be afraid.
>
> John 14:27

"Peace" in this passage doesn't just mean peace, but also harmony, security, safety, prosperity, and happiness – because peace and harmony make and keep things safe and

---

[39] Plantinga, Cornelius. *Not the Way It's Supposed to Be: A Breviary of Sin*, William B Eerdmans Publishing Co, 1995.

prosperous.[40] As Christians, peace also comes because we are assured of our salvation and have a secure eternal future.

Maintaining our peace is worth pursuing because it is a lifestyle that is on offer to us all. It is no surprise that our peace is attacked through worry and anxiety as it aims to undermine our confidence in Jesus and ourselves. Proverbs says "Above all else, guard your heart, for everything you do flows from it." (Prv. 4:23).

The Hebrew words in this passage are tôṣā'ôṯ and ḥay, which describe a source and springs of life that flows from within us.[41] Western cultural historically describes the heart as the source of our emotions. This verse encourages us to be both vigilant and diligent in guarding our emotions. We can learn to protect our internal world from unhealthy emotions.

The apostle Paul tells us how to do this: "Do not be anxious about anything, but in every situation, by prayer and petition, with thanksgiving, present your requests to God. And the peace of God, which transcends all understanding, will guard your hearts and your minds in Christ Jesus." (Phil. 4:6-7).

Challenging our worries

During our lives, we have both spent too much time worrying. Many of us worry about what other people think about us, not having enough money, our emotional issues, our loved ones, and maybe whether our lives have any significance. Despite this, does worrying help solve anything?

---

[40] eirēnē, Strong's G1515
[41] Strong's H844; Strong's H2416

Researcher Lucas LaFreniere, Ph.D. said, "This is what breaks my heart about worry. It makes you miserable in the present moment to try and prevent misery in the future. For chronic worriers, this process leads them to be continually distressed all their lives in order to avoid later events that never happen. Worry sucks the joy out of the 'here and now."

In his study on worry, 91.4 percent of participant's worries never happened.[42] The study also found that the more a participant accepted that their worries weren't likely to happen, the more their anxiety decreased. Challenging our worries with objective evidence means worry and anxiety can decrease.

Further, the study found that the participants "were realizing their worries were illogical, upsetting, and screwing with their thinking process and happiness, and ultimately were 'for nothing.'" Lucas LaFreniere said that his participants realised that "Their worries weren't worth the trouble they caused."

In another study, for those worries that did happen, 79 percent of participants discovered either they could handle the difficulty better than expected, or the difficulty taught them a lesson worth learning.[43] Overall this study showed that 97 percent of what we worry about is based upon exaggerations and misconceptions.

So when Jesus says to us "Do not worry about your life, what you will eat or drink; or about your body, what you will wear." (Mt. 6:25) he means it! He can provide for us. Rather our focus should be on seeking first his kingdom and his righteousness because if we do, he promises to take care of our needs (Mt. 6:28-34).

---

[42] LaFreniere, Lucas S. "Exposing Worry's Deceit: Percentage of Untrue Worries in Generalized Anxiety Disorder Treatment". *Science Direct.*
https://www.sciencedirect.com/science/article/abs/pii/S0005789419300826
[43] Leahy, Robert. *The Worry Cure.* Harmony, 2006.

DO NOT WORRY

After all, worrying does not help at all, it is a complete waste of time and emotion. Fear deceives us and wants to lead us down an unhelpful path, affirming our reasons for not feeling safe. It wants to convince us that we are subject to it, rather than shalom. As Jesus put it "Can any one of you by worrying add a single hour to your life?" (Mt. 6:27).

The internal clutter of worry and anxiety can stop us from living in the more of God. Rather than our thoughts being centred on Jesus' love and priorities, they are focused on fear. Persistent worrying and anxiety can significantly hinder our relationship with God and the fruitfulness of our Christian lives.

Writer and actor George Burns said, "If you ask what is the single most important key to longevity, I would have to say it is avoiding worry, stress and tension." If we want to run our Christian race to get the prize (1 Cor. 9:24), we need to be intentional in dealing with worry and anxiety. Being like Jesus means we will not worry.

Is worry something that is stopping you making space for Jesus?

Reflection

Consider these verses:

> *I tell you, do not worry about your life, what you will eat or drink; or about your body, what you will wear. Is not life more than food, and the body more than clothes? Look at the birds of the air; they do not sow or reap or store away in barns, and yet your heavenly Father feeds them. Are you not much more valuable than they? Can any one of you by worrying add a single hour to your life?*

> *And why do you worry about clothes? See how the flowers of the field grow. They do not labour or spin. Yet I tell you that not even Solomon in all his splendour was dressed like one of these. If that is how God clothes the grass of the field, which is here today and tomorrow is thrown into the fire, will he not much more clothe you—you of little faith?*

> *So do not worry, saying, 'What shall we eat?' or 'What shall we drink?' or 'What shall we wear?' For the pagans run after all these things, and your heavenly Father knows that you need them. But seek first his kingdom and his righteousness, and all these things will be given to you as well. Therefore do not worry about tomorrow, for tomorrow will worry about itself. Each day has enough trouble of its own.*

Matthew 6:25-34

Ask Father God:

- Lord, show me why I worry and what I am afraid of. What is your perspective on these things?
- Lord, how can I tangibly experience more of your love and peace?
- Lord, what support from others do I need to help me get free from worry and anxiety?

Prayer:

Father God, thank you I have been adopted as your child and into your kingdom. I pray that you will help me deal with the roots of my worry and anxiety and develop a lifestyle of peace.

To do:

- Meditate daily on the verses mentioned in this chapter to develop new truths and perspectives.
- Encourage yourself that you are a child of God and that anxiety does not have to have a hold on you.
- If your anxiety is persistent, severe or life-limiting, you may need to seek professional help to resolve it.

Further reading:

- Romans 12:1-2
- Ephesians 4:22-24
- Galatians 5

BE QUICK TO FORGIVE

To forgive is to set a prisoner free and discover that the prisoner was you.
(Lewis B. Smedes, Theologian)

"If I didn't leave my bitterness and hatred behind, I'd still be in prison"

Nelson Mandela was a South African anti-apartheid activist and politician who became the first black president of South Africa. His journey was far from easy – he experienced racism, bans on public speaking, harassment, and imprisonment. In June 1964 he was found guilty of sabotage and conspiracy to violently overthrow the government.

He stayed in prison for 27 years, often in poor conditions, having to perform forced labour and was regularly placed in solitary confinement. His mother and firstborn son died whilst he was imprisoned and he was forbidden to attend the funerals. He was rarely able to see his wife and his daughters first visited him in 1975, after he had been imprisoned for over ten years.

An escape plan was developed but was abandoned after it was infiltrated by State Security, who hoped Mandela could be shot during the escape. Despite an international campaign and foreign pressure, the government refused his release. He was part of the ANC, which at the time was considered a terrorist organisation.

Nelson Mandela had many reasons not to forgive those who had treated him so badly. His experiences could have left him understandably full of hatred and wanting revenge. Yet he saw forgiveness as the only way forward. He said:

> "Resentment is like drinking poison and then hoping it will kill your enemies."

When Nelson Mandela left prison he said:

> "As I walked out the door toward the gate that would lead to my freedom, I knew if I didn't leave my bitterness and hatred behind, I'd still be in prison."

Instead of revenge, he wanted a multicultural democracy and saw national reconciliation as the primary task of his presidency.[44]

Forgiveness in the Bible

If you have been offended by someone's words and actions, you are not alone. If you struggle to forgive someone for hurting you, that sentiment is shared by many. However, when Jesus was dying on the cross, he forgave those who were crucifying him (Lk. 23:34). When he did this, was he demonstrating something profound about forgiveness?

The word 'forgive' is defined as "to stop blaming or being angry with someone for something that person has done."[45] The Hebrews words aphiēmi, nāśā' and charizomai also include release from imprisonment, letting go, keeping no longer,

---

[44] Sampson, Anthony. *Mandela: The Authorised Biography*. HarperCollins, 2011.
[45] Cambridge Dictionary. https://dictionary.cambridge.org/dictionary/english/forgive

pardon of sins, giving freely, taking away, showing oneself gracious, and graciously restoring one to another.[46]

The word forgive, and its linguistic derivations, are mentioned over 136 times in the Bible and are included in nearly half of its books.[47] It is included in all book categories of the Bible, namely books on law, poetry, prophecy, gospels and epistles. Jesus' teaching, parables and discussions about forgiveness occur forty times in the gospels.

Forgiveness is central to the Bible's message because it is rooted in the character of God. The Psalms describe God as "forgiving and good" (Ps. 86:5), who "forgives all your sins" (Ps. 103:3) and with whom "there is forgiveness" (Ps. 130:4). Daniel says in a prayer to God that he "is merciful and forgiving, even though we have rebelled against him" (Dan. 9:9).

God does not hide his forgiving nature in the Bible, nor does he hide the importance of our need to forgive others. As children of God, we get to "participate in the divine nature" (2 Pet. 1:4) so that we can mirror God's nature to others. His nature can become our nature, his ability to forgive can become our ability to forgive.

God's nature is clear from the beginning of the Bible, as it is described in the second mention of the word forgive. When Moses encountered God on Mount Sinai, God described himself as "the compassionate and gracious God, slow to anger, abounding in love and faithfulness, maintaining love to thousands, and forgiving wickedness, rebellion and sin." (Ex. 34:6-7).

---

[46] Strong's G863; Strong's H5375; Strong's G5483
[47] 31 of the 66 Bible books

The first mention of the word 'forgive' in the Bible is at the end of the story of Joseph in Egypt. Out of jealousy, his brothers betrayed him and sold him to merchants, who then sold him as a slave to Pharoh's household. Joseph later was put in prison when he was falsely accused by Potiphar's wife (Gen. 39).

The life story of Joseph is a statement story about forgiveness. contained within Genesis, the first book of the Bible. We cannot escape the impact and significance of this. Through this story, God sovereignly saves many lives during a famine, but at its centre is the man Joseph, who demonstrates the importance and power of forgiveness.

After interpreting Pharaoh's dream, Joseph was released from prison and put in charge of the land of Egypt to plan for the forthcoming famine (Gen. 41). Due to the famine, Joseph's father Jacob sent his brothers to Egypt to buy grain. Following a second visit by his brothers to Egypt, Joseph reveals himself to his brothers. He was later reunited with his father Jacob (Gen. 46).

The time between Joseph being sold as a slave and being released from prison was 13 years. Joseph had many reasons to be angry with his brothers and he could, if he had wanted to, take revenge on them. When his father died, his brothers were concerned that Joseph would act badly towards them in their time following their father's death (Gen. 50).

So, they devised a plan by pretending that Jacob had left instructions before he died asking Joseph to forgive his brothers. When Joseph received their message he wept because he had no intention of harming them. Despite his mistreatment by his brothers and Potiphar, he still chose to forgive.

More profoundly he saw a different perspective of his circumstances. When his brothers threw themselves down in front of Joseph, expecting the worst, he spoke kindly to them "You intended to harm me, but God intended it for good to accomplish what is now being done, the saving of many lives." (Gen. 50:20).

The story of Joseph shows the ability of God to work through the bad decisions of human beings to bring about a greater good. This story was made into a movie in 1995 and multiple musicals since 1972.[48] Taking into account amateur productions it is estimated that this story has been seen by more than 200 million people.[49]

Jesus teaching on forgiveness

When Jesus taught us to pray, he provided a model prayer that is referred to as the Lord's Prayer. The prayer includes "Forgive us our sins, for we also forgive everyone who sins against us." (Lk. 11:4). Jesus expects that when we ask God to forgive our sins, we are maintaining a lifestyle of forgiving others.

Forgiveness is not an optional extra for a Christian, it is a lifestyle we adopt because we have been forgiven by God for our sins. Knowing that God has forgiven everything wrong we have ever said, thought or did, means we provide the same kindness to others. As the apostle Paul encourages us, loving others means we do not keep a record of wrongs (1 Cor. 13:5).

The cost Jesus paid when he died on the cross for our sins so we can all be forgiven was immense. When we grasp this, it

---

[48] The Guardian. "50 years of Joseph and the Amazing Technicolor Dreamcoat – in pictures". *The Guardian*. https://www.theguardian.com/stage/gallery/2019/mar/02/50-years-of-joseph-and-the-amazing-technicolor-dreamcoat-in-pictures
[49] Cox, Jonathan. "Joseph and the Amazing Technicolor Dreamcoat". *Stage Whispers*. https://www.stagewhispers.com.au/reviews/joseph-and-amazing-technicolor-dreamcoat-11

makes sense that God expects us to forgive others. Yet when we are deeply offended and hurt by another human being, it can be hard to forgive. That is why Jesus recognises this and he takes the time to explain its importance.

When Peter asked Jesus how many times he should forgive someone, he suggested that seven times was a reasonable amount. Jesus has a different perspective and says to Peter "I tell you, not seven times, but seventy-seven times." (Mt. 18:22). Here, Jesus is perhaps not introducing a higher limit, but is referring to the story of Cain and Abel.

In Genesis 4, Cain kills his brother Abel, which is the first murder in the Bible. Cain then has to leave the Lord's presence but is marked by God to protect him from being killed. God gives him the promise that "anyone who kills Cain will suffer vengeance seven times over." (Gen. 4:15), which is amazingly gracious of God considering Cain's sin.

Lamech is born five generations later and says to his wives "I have killed a man for wounding me, a young man for injuring me. If Cain is avenged seven times, then Lamech seventy-seven times." (Gen. 4:23-24). Jesus is contrasting forgiveness to Lamech's need for his relative Cain's death to be avenged.

When we are hurt by someone it can cause us to want revenge so that we can in some way punish them for what they have done wrong. Jesus then continues to tell a parable of a man who has a great debt cancelled, but who then does not cancel a much smaller debt that is owed to him by another man. The man is then handed over to the jailer until his debt is paid (Mt. 18:23-34).

Jesus concludes this parable with this powerful statement "This is how my heavenly Father will treat each of you unless you forgive your brother or sister from your heart." (Mt. 18:35). When we do not forgive someone, we create an illusion that we are punishing the offender, but in fact we find ourselves in a prison, punishing ourselves instead.

Jesus' teaching on prayer underlines this further, he says "For if you forgive other people when they sin against you, your heavenly Father will also forgive you. But if you do not forgive others their sins, your Father will not forgive your sins." (Mt. 6:14-15). If we want to be forgiven by God, then we have to forgive others.

Forgiveness is for our benefit. It removes any hatred, bitterness and vengeance we hold and let fester in our hearts and minds for a person who has hurt or offended us. Studies have found that more forgiving people "tend to be more satisfied with their lives and to have less depression, anxiety, stress, anger and hostility."[50]

Jesus understands this and it is why he uses the parable of the unmerciful servant to communicate it so clearly. If someone offered you a daily poison that would over time damage your body, you would not take it. Yet when we do not forgive, all the anger and resentment in our emotions start to poison our wellbeing.

Forgiveness needs to be a lifestyle and is something we may need to do regularly for particular people. Jesus said:

> "If your brother or sister sins against you, rebuke them; and if they repent, forgive them.

---

[50] John Hopkins Medicine. "Forgiveness: Your Health Depends on It". *John Hopkins Medicine.* https://www.hopkinsmedicine.org/health/wellness-and-prevention/forgiveness-your-health-depends-on-it

> Even if they sin against you seven times in a day and seven times come back to you saying 'I repent,' you must forgive them."

Luke 17:3-4

Is forgiveness a weakness?

Amy Orr-Ewing, author and theologian, says in her blog "We seem to have lost the art of forgiveness in 21st century Britain. Instead, cancel culture is all around us. From the impetus to punish a person whose ideas or behaviour we disagree with by shunning the transgressor, to lobbying to get a person fired, or black-listed from speaking, publishing or lecturing, cancel culture thrives."[51]

Cancel culture is a phrase used to refer to "a culture in which those who are deemed to have acted or spoken in an unacceptable manner are ostracized, boycotted, or shunned."[52] Forgiveness is rejected as a weakness by supporters of cancel culture because they believe it denies the seriousness of injustice and wrongdoing.

Mahatma Gandhi disagreed. He said "The weak can never forgive. Forgiveness is the attribute of the strong." The reason forgiveness can be hard is because injustice and wrongdoing can be serious. During the process of forgiveness, the one who forgives typically acknowledges the seriousness of the wrongdoing as they can forgive.

---

[51] Orr-Ewing, Amy. "At the start of 2022 will cancel culture continue to shape our common life?". *Amy Orr-Ewing*. https://www.amyorr-ewing.com/blog/start-2022-will-cancel-culture-continue-shape-our-common-life
[52] en.wikipedia.org/wiki/Cancel_culture

BE QUICK TO FORGIVE

Desmond Tutu won a Nobel Peace Prize in 1984 for opposition to apartheid and led the country's Truth and Reconciliation Commission. He wrote:

> "Forgiving is not forgetting; it's actually remembering ... and not using your right to hit back. It's a second chance for a new beginning. And the remembering part is particularly important. Especially if you don't want to repeat what happened."

Malala Yousafzai, a female education activist, said "Whatever hatred you have against this person, it's not going to solve any of the problems... I can take my revenge by educating girls. That's the best way to fight back." [53]

We don't have to hate those who have hurt us.

For most of us who have been offended and hurt, there is often a desire to see justice. When Jesus died on the cross taking away the sin of the world, God judged that injustice and wrongdoing are serious offences against him and his creation. His answer was for his Son to take on himself the punishment we deserved (Rom. 3:23-26).

Jesus has taken the punishment for the way others may have treated us. We therefore cannot say we will not forgive until the offender is brought to justice, because Jesus took the offender's place. So when Jesus asks us to forgive, it is in the context that justice has already taken place through his substitution.

It is also important not to miss that there is only one judge – God himself. Only God can truly judge an offender's motive

---

[53] Wake, Heather. "Malala revealed that she spoke with her attackers—and it's a masterclass in forgiveness". *Up Worthy*. https://www.upworthy.com/malala-forgives-her-attackers

and actions. We may accurately understand them in some cases, but in others, we may overlook or exaggerate them. In all cases, God has fairly judged their actions and sent his son Jesus to die in their place.

Jesus is also clear that receiving forgiveness can be dependent on forgiving others by saying:

> "Do not judge, and you will not be judged. Do not condemn, and you will not be condemned. Forgive, and you will be forgiven. Give, and it will be given to you. A good measure, pressed down, shaken together and running over, will be poured into your lap. For with the measure you use, it will be measured to you."
>
> Luke 6:37-38

Ouch! Did you grasp Jesus' words here? Giving mercy and forgiveness to others means we will receive mercy and forgiveness from others. If we want a good measure of more of God in our lives then we need to forgive others. His words are crystal clear, but do we hear them and take them seriously, especially when we have been deeply hurt by someone?

Don't rush on, pause for a moment. Let Jesus' words impact you. Consider them, think them through. Are you living them or are you holding unforgiveness in your heart? The apostle Paul encourages us to examine ourselves when we take communion (1 Cor. 11:23-34) so that we would avoid further sin and judgment.

When we are unforgiving it can fill our internal world with anger, resentment and even hatred towards someone. We can become offended by their words and actions, and often rehearse them in our thoughts and feelings, in an attempt to justify our

unforgiveness. Such a heart posture is incompatible with asking God for more of him in our lives.

When God forgave the human race for its sin through the death of his son Jesus, he was showing his true nature. As his children, he wants us to represent him and show his forgiveness to others. Forgiving others as he forgave us is *the* standard for us as Christians and part of the new covenant (Eph. 4:32 & Mt. 26:28).

The story in the Bible that highlights a need for justice is when a woman is caught in adultery:

> At dawn he appeared again in the temple courts, where all the people gathered round him, and he sat down to teach them. The teachers of the law and the Pharisees brought in a woman caught in adultery. They made her stand before the group and said to Jesus, 'Teacher, this woman was caught in the act of adultery. In the Law Moses commanded us to stone such women. Now what do you say?' They were using this question as a trap, in order to have a basis for accusing him.
>
> But Jesus bent down and started to write on the ground with his finger. When they kept on questioning him, he straightened up and said to them, 'Let any one of you who is without sin be the first to throw a stone at her.' Again he stooped down and wrote on the ground.
>
> At this, those who heard began to go away one at a time, the older ones first, until only Jesus was left, with the woman still standing there. Jesus straightened up and asked her, 'Woman, where are they? Has no one condemned you?'
>
> 'No one, sir,' she said.

> 'Then neither do I condemn you,' Jesus declared. 'Go now and leave your life of sin.'
>
> John 8:2-11

John tells us that this moment was created by the teachers of the law and the Pharisees to try to trap Jesus. The woman caught in adultery finds herself a pawn in their plans. She would have felt embarrassed, ashamed and in fear for her life. In a male-dominated society, she would have felt the impact of the power imbalance, knowing they would have stoned her to death.

Yet in this moment, Jesus does something remarkable. Through his question, he creates awareness that all have sinned and all deserve death under Moses' Law. After all the people have left, he treats the woman with dignity but implores her to leave her life of sin because it can have serious consequences. Without his intervention, she would almost certainly have died that day.

When we are offended and hurt, we may be tempted to act like the crowd in the story and demand that the offender gets justice. What Jesus wants us to understand, is that we also have sinned and therefore we face the same judgement as the offender. It may be in our eyes that the sin of the offender is worse than our own sin, but nevertheless, we are all guilty of sin.

Jesus' words are a great leveller and can help us understand that it is therefore reasonable to forgive others because we all have faults and we all hurt people through our words and actions. Some actions may be significantly greater than others and have more devastating consequences, but we are all guilty of breaking God's laws (Jas. 2:10).

Mark Twain, writer and lecturer, put it like this: "Forgiveness is the fragrance that the violet sheds on the heel that has crushed it." If we are hurt or offended by someone, that is not meant to be the destination. Jesus encourages us to forgive for our own benefit but also to show love because those who are forgiven more will love more (Lk. 7:47).

Forgiving their captors

In our early twenties, we got to meet some church leaders from an underground church abroad. They described to us their imprisonment, hard labour, frequent beatings, and punishments that they experienced in their decades in prison. They also spoke about what God had done in and through them whilst they were in prison.

What struck us was that they were not bitter about their experience. They were the most godly and well-adjusted people we have ever met. They had forgiven their captors and their hearts were full of affection for Jesus because of the love they had experienced from him whilst in prison. They just radiated the love of God.

They had moved on from their prison experience and were actively teaching and equipping the underground church. They were not stuck in the past but were very much in the present moment. They were full of thankfulness, kindness, and humility, and still in love with Jesus. Jesus had been a greater influence on them than their difficult experience of prison.

They were an example to us in many ways and we have never forgotten the short time we had with them. They seemed to have so little clutter in their lives. If we don't forgive, unforgiveness can create significant internal clutter in our lives and stop us from experiencing all that God has planned for us.

How do we forgive others, ourselves and even God?

During our lifetime, we have had many opportunities to be offended by some people's words and actions towards us. We have been lied to, threatened, mistreated, ignored, overlooked, maligned, falsely accused, misunderstood, and manipulated. Yet we have learned that in the end, the only way to be free is to forgive.

We will know if we need to forgive someone if when their name is mentioned we feel wounded, angry, or resentful. This may also happen when we meet them or in a quiet moment, our emotions are focused on the pain they have caused us. We may also feel hatred and the need for revenge.

If this is the case, we have a choice to forgive them. We may feel we should resent rather than forgive them. If we forgive them it may feel that we have let them off their offence. It could be that we feel they don't deserve to be forgiven, after all, they are the wrongdoers. It is among these conflicted feelings that we get to choose to forgive.

Forgiveness is not just about others but also applies to us as well. We should apply the same grace to others that we do to ourselves.[54] If there is any area of shame, regret or sorrow where we feel we have let ourselves down, we need to forgive ourselves. This may be for something we have done or something we should have done, but didn't.

In terms of our relationship with God, God cannot be guilty of wrongdoing. Therefore the process is not one of forgiveness as such. However if we perceive that he has in some way let us

---

[54] Good Thinking. "The 4 Rs of self-forgiveness". *Good Thinking*. https://www.good-thinking.uk/blog/4-rs-self-forgiveness

down, we may feel hurt or offended by him because he may not have acted in the way we wanted him to.[55] Holding onto resentment or offence towards God is something we need to let go of.

The process outlined below applies to all these three scenarios (i.e. others, ourselves and God). It may help to write down your answers.

1. Thank God that your sins are forgiven and ask God to comfort you. You may find it helpful to draw near to God in sung worship.

2. Fully acknowledge the situation that caused you offence and hurt. Be real about your emotions, as these can help you identify what you need to forgive.

3. Identify the person or people that were the cause of offence and hurt. Be as specific as you can as to how each person upset you.

4. Ask God if your assessment is realistic, checking that you have not underestimated or exaggerated any of the impact of the offence and hurt.

5. Decide that you will choose to no longer hold onto any anger or resentment towards the people who caused you hurt.

6. Give up your right for personal revenge, acknowledging that Jesus has taken to the cross the sins of the people who hurt you.

---

[55] If you want to explore forgiveness further, we would recommend the book Kendall, R.T., *Total Forgiveness: Achieving God's Greatest Challenge*, Hodder & Stoughton, 2003

7. For each person on your list say out loud to God their name and specifically what you are forgiving them for.

After completing this process, if you have truly forgiven people, then at this point you can choose to move on and leave your hurt behind. If there is a specific situation or person whom you are finding hard to forgive, it may help to go through this process with a trusted Christian friend or pastor.

If you have experienced trauma through people's wrongdoing, it may mean you need to process and untangle some of that hurt before you can forgive. If that applies to you, we recommend reading the chapter *Be Patient In Affliction* and then revisiting the forgiveness process.

Well done if you have just forgiven someone or yourself, it can be hard to do so. We encourage you to make forgiveness a lifestyle so that unforgiveness does not build up over time. This is the best way to keep our lives free of unforgiving clutter.

Will we make space for Jesus by forgiving those we need to?

Reflection

Consider these verses:

> *If we claim to be without sin, we deceive ourselves and the truth is not in us. If we confess our sins, he is faithful and just and will forgive us our sins and purify us from all unrighteousness. If we claim we have not sinned, we make him out to be a liar and his word is not in us.*
>
> 1 John 1:8-10

Ask Father God:

- Lord, who do I need to forgive?
- Lord, is there anything that I have not forgiven myself for?
- Lord, am I are struggling to forgive someone? If so, why is that?

Prayer:

> *Thank you Father God that you have forgiven me. Thank you Jesus for your example of how you forgave people. Enable me to live a lifestyle of forgiveness.*

To do:

- Using the process outlined above, forgive those who have hurt or offended you.

- Make a list of things that people have forgiven you for. If you haven't already done so, why not thank them?
- Set aside some time to meditate over passages of the Bible that speak about forgiveness.

Further reading:

- Genesis 4
- Matthew 18:21-35
- Psalm 32

DO NOT BE DISMAYED

Disappointment is a stepping stone to resilience. It toughens you up and prepares you for the challenges that lie ahead.
(Michelle Obama, First Lady, Attorney and Author)

"I give up"

In our mid-twenties, we moved towns and churches in response to a prophetic word we were given. We quickly fell in love with the town we moved to and also the hospitable church we joined. We simply loved life; what could go wrong? We owned a house in the place we had moved from and wanted to buy a house in the new town we were in.

We found a house in the new town and decided it was the one. It was ideal for the family that we planned to have one day. We made an offer for the house and it was accepted. We then waited for a buyer for our old house, but the sale fell through twice over a period of a year and a half.

We became disappointed and discouraged. We felt that God had led us to buy the house, but it was not panning out as we had hoped. The feelings we had seemed to sap our confidence in God for a good outcome. On the way to church one Sunday morning, I (Mark) said to Fiona "I give up going after this house".

During the church meeting, a friend came up to Mark and asked if they could pray for him. This particular friend did not know the situation he was going through. She prayed hope and encouragement over Mark and it felt like his emotions and connection with God were reset. Mark started to believe again that God had a plan for us.

The new house we wanted to buy was near where we were renting a property. So on the way home, Mark would walk via the house and pray that God would give it to us. He did this for many months, not knowing how long it would take. A little later we received the good news that we had a buyer for our old house.

The next weekend we went straight to the estate agent to make an offer on the new house, for the third time. Despite having withdrawn our offer twice, the house owner accepted our offer. The house-buying journey ended in celebration and delight, but we found the journey emotionally draining.

Looking back, we can see God's providence in the journey and the invitations to trust in his sovereignty. Because the whole process took so much longer than we had anticipated, the house selling price had reduced, as had the mortgage interest rates (by a third), which saved us a lot of money. Even so, at the time we had struggled to deal with disappointment.

Not being able to buy the house that we want is unlikely to be the moment in life that causes us the greatest disappointment. Yet for us, it was the first time that disappointment affected our relationship with God. We began to understand how disappointment can negatively affect our connection with Jesus.

DO NOT BE DISMAYED

The power of disappointment

At the start of the classic Christmas movie, *It's a Wonderful Life*, God is having a conversation with Joseph in heaven about the main character George Bailey, because many of his family and friends are praying for him. God calls for an angel called Clarence to help George. Clarence arrives and asks God if George needs help because he is sick. God replies "No, worse; he's discouraged."

Disappointment often leads to discouragement, both of which are very powerful emotions. Disappointment is defined as "the unhappiness or discouragement that results when your hopes or expectations have not been satisfied, or someone or something that is not as good as you had hoped or expected."[56]

Proverbs puts it like this: "Hope deferred makes the heart sick, but a longing fulfilled is a tree of life." (Prv. 13:12). King Solomon also said our heart is the springs of life and everything we do flows from it (Prv. 4:23). "Heart" in this passage represents our soul, mind, will, emotions, and passions.[57]

That is why the Bible's wisdom is to guard our hearts "above all else" (Prv. 4:23). This is a powerful statement, that in the context of all his wisdom, the most important thing is to guard our heart. "Guard your heart" means watching, preserving, blockading, and keeping from danger.[58]

If we don't guard our hearts from disappointment and discouragement, it negatively affects our thinking, emotions, conscience, determination, character, passions and courage. In

---

[56] Cambridge Dictionary. https://dictionary.cambridge.org/dictionary/english/disappointment
[57] lēb, Strong's H3820
[58] nāsar, Strong's H5341

effect, both disappointment and discouragement can powerfully negatively affect us and change who we are from the inside out.

We can't avoid being impacted by disappointments in our lives but we can avoid them from affecting the core of our being. If we recognise how detrimental both disappointment and discouragement can be, we will work hard to guard the core of our being from getting damaged by these emotions.

In our experience, if we become disappointed and don't resolve it, it can eat away at our hope, confidence and connection with God. Over time, our chief emotion will no longer be towards God but get drawn towards temporal things that provide us with short-term comfort, distraction, meaning and an inferior sense of purpose.

This is why disappointment can be dangerous, it is like an anaesthetic that results in insensitivity to God. It can start very subtly, and its effect can be at first unnoticeable, but over time it will pollute our springs of life and dull our sensitivity towards him. It can become a cul-de-sac, where we stop seeking and pursuing God and our destiny in him.

We can get drawn into either neutral or unhealthy activities to try to deal with our unresolved disappointment, which typically is either distraction or escapism. It could be as innocent as watching movies or eating our favourite food. Whatever it is, our chief passion is no longer Jesus and his kingdom.

We may also stop praying for and encouraging our Christian brothers and sisters, or we may even withdraw from the body of Christ. We may make little time to share our faith or help the marginalised because we have unresolved pain in our hearts. We are likely to spend less time with Father God and worshipping him. Pain, disappointment and discouragement create a tendency to withdraw.

Our modern world is full of distractions which are primarily found digitally via our mobile phones. We can waste vast amounts of time on social media, music, gaming and video streaming services. Though they can be entertaining, they are unlikely to provide an antidote for our disappointment.

In the UK, people spend an average of 4.8 hours a day on their mobile phones, which is equivalent to a third of their waking time.[59] In the US, time spent with non-voice activities on mobile phones is 4.6 hours.[60] People in Brazil, Indonesia and South Korea surpassed five hours per day.

When it comes to streaming services, daily time spent on Netflix is 3.2 hours a day, with the average weekly time spent worldwide with online video in 2022 being 19 hours.[61] When it comes to social media, worldwide the average person spends 2 hours and 31 minutes scrolling through social media channels.[62]

What if we compare time on a screen with time spent in prayer? In the US, "among those who pray, the typical prayer lasts around a minute or two for nearly 40 percent of Americans and a little over 5 percent of Americans pray for half an hour or

---

[59] Wakefield, Jane. "People devote third of waking time to mobile apps". *BBC News.* https://www.bbc.co.uk/news/technology-59952557

[60] Statista. "Time spent with nonvoice activities on mobile phones every day in the United States from 2019 to 2024". *Statista.* https://www.statista.com/statistics/1045353/mobile-device-daily-usage-time-in-the-us

[61] Cook, Sam. "Netflix statistics: How many movies and TV shows do they have? 2024". *CompariTech.* https://www.comparitech.com/blog/vpn-privacy/netflix-statistics-facts-figures; Statista. "Average weekly time spent with online video worldwide from 2018 to 2023". Statista. https://www.statista.com/statistics/611707/online-video-time-spent

[62] Moody, Rebecca. "Screen Time Statistics: Average Screen Time by Country". *CompariTech.* https://www.comparitech.com/tv-streaming/screen-time-statistics

more whenever they pray."[63] In the UK, most people pray on the go, rather than making it a dedicated activity.[64]

We can spend more time entertaining ourselves than spending time with God. If we don't develop a regular connection with God, when disappointment comes it may be hard to deal with. Disappointment and discouragement can become significant internal clutter in our lives that can choke the life of God in us, if left unresolved.

A God of comfort

When we are disappointed or discouraged we need comfort from God, which he delights to give. When we come to God, he will not push us away but give us the Holy Spirit who is the Advocate and Comforter. The comfort that comes in these moments from the Holy Spirit reminds us who God is and brings us peace:

> But the Advocate, the Holy Spirit, whom the Father will send in my name, will teach you all things and will remind you of everything I have said to you.
>
> Peace I leave with you; my peace I give you. I do not give to you as the world gives. Do not let your hearts be troubled and do not be afraid.
>
> John 14:26-27

---

[63] Froese, Paul. "Prayer in America: A Detailed Analysis of the Various Dimensions of Prayer". *Wiley Online.*
https://onlinelibrary.wiley.com/doi/full/10.1111/jssr.12810#:~:text=Among%20those%20who%20pray%2C%20the,pray%20(see%20Figure%202).

[64] Tearfund. "Half of adults in the UK say that they pray". *Tearfund.*
https://www.tearfund.org/stories/media/press-releases/half-of-adults-in-the-uk-say-that-they-pray

DO NOT BE DISMAYED

God's comfort is the remedy we need to restore our springs of life. His comfort will invigorate our souls and bring a fresh impartation of love and hope. His peace will settle our troubled hearts. We can be confident in God's ability to solve our disappointment and discouragement.

It is important to realise that God does not become discouraged in his purpose to work in and through us (Isa. 42:4). He also has the solution to our discouragement – courage, which is often what we need when he asks us to do something. There are multiple examples of this in the Bible, where people need to choose courage to fulfil their destiny.[65]

Discouragement is a common tactic of the enemy to try and stop people from fulfilling what God has called them to do. When Ezra and Nehemiah led the rebuilding of the temple mid-5th century BC, "the peoples around them set out to discourage the people of Judah and make them afraid to go on building." (Ezra 4:4). This caused the rebuilding work to stop for many decades.

Paul says he was not unaware of Satan's schemes and neither should we be (2 Cor. 2:11). We should expect to face discouragement and learn how to overcome it. Joshua is a good example for us, he was told by God three times to be courageous. When we are courageous we can trust that God is truly with us (Jos. 1:6, 7 & 9).

When God speaks multiple times to Joshua to "be courageous", he is saying be strong, alert, brave, and strengthen oneself.[66] When the disciples see Jesus walking on water during a storm, he doesn't say stop worrying, he tells them to "take courage" (Mt. 14:27).[67]

---

[65] For example, Duet. 1:19-21, Duet.3:17-9, 1 Chr. 22:11-13 and 2 Chr. 20:16-17
[66] 'āmēṣ, Strong's H553
[67] tharseō, Strong's G2293

Courage is not a feeling, rather it "is the quality shown by someone who decides to do something difficult or dangerous, even though they may be afraid."[68] Courage is the choice we choose to make despite the circumstances we are in. It may mean we need to confront pain, uncertainty, or intimidation.

Saying I don't *feel* courageous misses the point, because it is making a choice, even though we may feel afraid. When we feel discouraged we need to take a brave step forward, even though our feelings may be at odds with this choice. It is the same when we are disappointed, we need to take a step in the direction that will lead towards hope.

This does not mean denying our feelings, after all, the Beach Ball metaphor in psychology encourages us to engage our negative feelings rather than trying to push them down. This is akin to trying to push an inflated beach ball underwater, which requires huge amounts of energy and is almost impossible.[69]

It is better to let the air out of the ball and deflate it, which represents processing our unhelpful feelings using a variety of psychological methods. Acknowledging the reality of our feelings, such as discouragement, is a more effective way to make a courageous step forward.

We do not deny the reality of the situation we are in, but rather despite the circumstances, we can trust God to make a way forward that we can walk in. Taking a step forward in courage also means we begin to trust God with our future, believing in something better than the situation we are in.

---

[68] Collins. https://www.collinsdictionary.com/dictionary/english/courage
[69] Sabater, Valeria. "The Beach Ball Metaphor for Emotional Regulation". *Exploring Your Mind.* exploringyourmind.com/the-beach-ball-metaphor-for-emotional-regulation

Jesus: a man of courage

If we want an example of courage to inspire us, then there is none better than Jesus. Jesus was with God in the beginning, and all things were made through him (Jn. 1:1-2). Jesus was also human and the Gospels and Hebrews tell us that he shared in our humanity (Jn. 1:14 and Heb. 2:14).

Jesus knew he would suffer death on the cross. Despite this, he willingly chose to become a man and through his death redeem humanity from sin. We rightly rejoice that through this act of sacrifice, we are forgiven and reconciled to God (2 Cor. 5:18-20). Yet do we truly comprehend his courage (Lk 9:51)?

When Jesus rose from the dead and ascended into heaven, the book of Hebrews described him as a great high priest:

> Therefore, since we have a great high priest who has ascended into heaven, Jesus the Son of God, let us hold firmly to the faith we profess.
>
> For we do not have a high priest who is unable to feel sympathy for our weaknesses, but we have one who has been tempted in every way, just as we are – yet he did not sin.
>
> Let us then approach God's throne of grace with confidence, so that we may receive mercy and find grace to help us in our time of need.
>
> Hebrews 4:14-16

Because help from Jesus is always available, we can choose to hold firmly to our faith, even when life is difficult. Jesus' example of courage is helpful to us because we can approach

God in confidence. Our great high priest understands our emotions, weaknesses and struggles.

The courage we require is to re-engage with God and have confidence that he can lead us out of discouragement and disappointment. Rather than escapism or distraction, the very thing we need to do is humble ourselves and seek comfort from God. If we have sought comfort in unhealthy places we can draw near in repentance.

Disappointment can be a powerful teacher

Author and researcher Brené Brown says "Disappointment is a powerful teacher. It reminds us to reassess our expectations and find strength in resilience." Author Eckhart Tolle says "Disappointment is a reminder that life doesn't always go as planned. Embrace the uncertainty, for it is what makes the journey worthwhile."

We can feel subject to disappointment as something that emotionally hurts us, or we can embrace it as a teacher to build resilience in us. This needs a different perspective and often requires us to step back and ask what we can learn from the disappointment we have experienced.

As a starting point, even though we may feel the emotions of disappointment, we can choose not to camp in them. The apostle Paul tells us "And we know that in all things God works for the good of those who love him, who have been called according to his purpose." (Rom. 8:28).

Being patient in God's providence to do us good through the circumstances we find ourselves in is a healthy focus, even if things don't work out as we had hoped. This way, we are more likely to keep our eyes fixed on Jesus. the author and perfecter of our faith, and less likely to stay problem-focused (Heb. 12:2).

Resilience means we are "able to be happy, successful, etc. again after something difficult or bad has happened."[70] We build our resilience over time through our experiences. It is like a muscle; the more we exercise it the stronger it grows. How we choose to react in difficult moments is what influences whether our resilience grows.

The American Psychological Association defines resilience as "the process and outcome of successfully adapting to difficult or challenging life experiences, especially through mental, emotional, and behavioural flexibility and adjustment to external and internal demands."[71] They also state that research shows that such skills can be cultivated and practised.

These skills can include healthy attitudes such as gratitude and compassion as well as taking a day at a time and remaining hopeful. Add courage to this list; the courage to stay connected with God and the courage to walk through disappointing emotions. As the apostle Paul says, "Stand firm in the faith; be courageous; be strong." (1 Cor. 16:13).

Thich Nhat Hanh, an author and peace activist, says "When disappointment knocks on your door, greet it with gratitude, for it reveals the gaps that need to be filled in order to grow." Disappointment and discouragement can enable God to work in us, as the apostle Paul says, "It is God who works in you to will and to act in order to fulfil his good purpose." (Phil. 2:13).

---

[70] Cambridge Dictionary, https://dictionary.cambridge.org/dictionary/english/resilient
[71] APA. "Resilience". *American Psychological Association.* www.apa.org/topics/resilience

Being disappointed with ourselves

When we feel like we have failed God, it can lead us to feel disappointed with ourselves and discouraged by it. It can also create distance in our relationship with God if we withdraw from him. Yet when we feel we have failed, Jesus invites us into a conversation to restore us. This is what Jesus did for Peter after he denied him three times following his arrest.

In 2020 we went to Israel to encounter its history, geography, and culture.[72] Whilst we were there we had several profound encounters with Jesus. One of these occurred when we visited the courtyard of the Church of St Peter in Gallicantu. This is one of the most likely locations for Caiaphas's palace, where Peter denied Jesus.

Peter's denial is recorded in all four gospels, and three of them record his bitter tears of remorse:

> Then seizing him, they led him away and took him into the house of the high priest. Peter followed at a distance. And when some there had kindled a fire in the middle of the courtyard and had sat down together, Peter sat down with them. A servant-girl saw him seated there in the firelight. She looked closely at him and said, 'This man was with him.'
>
> But he denied it. 'Woman, I don't know him,' he said.
>
> A little later someone else saw him and said, 'You also are one of them.'

---

[72] The Stones Cry Out. "Encounter Israel". *The Stones Cry Out*.
https://thestonescryout.org.uk/bible-lands-israel-2

'Man, I am not!' Peter replied.

About an hour later another asserted, 'Certainly this fellow was with him, for he is a Galilean.'

Peter replied, 'Man, I don't know what you're talking about!' Just as he was speaking, the cock crowed. The Lord turned and looked straight at Peter.

Then Peter remembered the word the Lord had spoken to him: 'Before the cock crows today, you will disown me three times.' And he went outside and wept bitterly.

Luke 22:54-62

The details in this story are really important as they are significant in the conversation Jesus later has with Peter, when he restores him. The courtyard of the Church of St Peter in Gallicantu is relatively small. Therefore it is likely that Jesus heard the conversation between Peter and the servant-girl, including Peter's three denials.

There was also a fire in the courtyard where Peter was sitting, so when Jesus looked at Peter after the cock crowed, he most likely would have looked at him across the top of the fire. Jesus would then have watched Peter stand up and leave the courtyard as he went outside and wept.

After Jesus' resurrection, he met his disciples several times. One particular meeting occurred by the Sea of Galilee, Peter and six of the other disciples had gone fishing at night. Early in the morning he stood on the shore and called out to them in the boat. Peter recognised him and swam to the shore.

Jesus is waiting for them on the beach and he has lit a fire to make breakfast cooking the fish they caught:

> Jesus said to them, 'Bring some of the fish you have just caught.' So Simon Peter climbed back into the boat and dragged the net ashore. It was full of large fish, 153, but even with so many the net was not torn.
>
> Jesus said to them, 'Come and have breakfast.' None of the disciples dared ask him, 'Who are you?' They knew it was the Lord. Jesus came, took the bread and gave it to them, and did the same with the fish. This was now the third time Jesus appeared to his disciples after he was raised from the dead.
>
> When they had finished eating, Jesus said to Simon Peter, 'Simon son of John, do you love me more than these?'
>
> 'Yes, Lord,' he said, 'you know that I love you.'
>
> Jesus said, 'Feed my lambs.'
>
> Again Jesus said, 'Simon son of John, do you love me?' He answered, 'Yes, Lord, you know that I love you.'
>
> Jesus said, 'Take care of my sheep.'
>
> The third time he said to him, 'Simon son of John, do you love me?'
>
> Peter was hurt because Jesus asked him the third time, 'Do you love me?' He said, 'Lord, you know all things; you know that I love you.'

Jesus said, 'Feed my sheep. Very truly I tell you, when you were younger you dressed yourself and went where you wanted; but when you are old you will stretch out your hands, and someone else will dress you and lead you where you do not want to go.' Jesus said this to indicate the kind of death by which Peter would glorify God.

Then he said to him, 'Follow me!'

John 21:10-19

The details between the two stories link together. Jesus asks him three times whether he loves him. This is the same number of times that Peter denied Jesus. It was also the third time that Jesus had appeared to his disciples. Jesus is asking Peter into a similar context that he denied him in, even down to the detail of having a conversation next to an open fire.

Peter found this conversation difficult. This was not just because Jesus asked him if he loved him the same number of his denials, but also because of the different words Jesus used for love. In the first two questions, Jesus uses the Greek word agapaō, whereas Peter replies using the Greek word phileō.[73]

These two words have different definitions. Agapaō denotes a divine self-sacrificial love whereas phileō denotes human love, more akin to a friendly affection.[74] This question seems very pertinent, especially as Jesus alludes to the fact that Peter will die in a way that will glorify Jesus.

---

[73] agapaō, Strong's G25;phileō, Strong's G5368
[74] Evans, Phil. "Agapaō and phileō". *Living Faith.* https://living-faith.org/2018/03/30/agapao-and-phileo

When Jesus asks Peter a third time if he loves him, he uses the word phileō, the same word Peter had used, which is why Peter likely felt hurt. It was like Jesus was asking him *how much* he loved him. When we find ourselves disappointed or discouraged, the key question that Jesus has for us is how much we love him?

Do we trust him for what he has planned for us? Are we confident that he can lead us out of this place of disappointment and discouragement? Do we have the same understanding of the future he had planned for us? Do we have the resilience needed for his plans for us? Will we follow him with an agapaō love?

It is as though Jesus re-creates this moment by the fire so he can restore Peter's relationship with him. Jesus may want to do the same with us if we have withdrawn, and it may be that Jesus asks us searching and difficult questions. Jesus may want to address the root of why we have become disappointed.

This root may be more about our faith and confidence in God than the specifics of the circumstance that causes us to be disappointed. It is such moments that reveal what we really believe about God and ourselves. We need to let Jesus ask us searching questions so he can deal with the root issues.

Jesus sets the scene to restore Peter, but Peter has to come and engage with him. It may be that Jesus is waiting for you to come and engage with him as the starting point of resolving your disappointment or discouragement. Jesus knows how we feel, and is waiting for us to meet him, so he can restore us.

Jesus just didn't meet Peter, slap him on the back in a friendly way and say "It's all right, I forgive you!". It needed a stretching conversation with Jesus to bring restoration. That is because it was not just about Peter's denial but also about his future. Jesus has a plan for Peter to have a key role in the early church but needs to restore him first.

Jesus was not just restoring Peter's dignity, identity and purpose, but also his destiny, which is described in two ways in this passage. Jesus asks him to feed and take care of his sheep and lambs, which is about how Peter will love Christians in the church. The other way is related to the miraculous catch of 153 fish.

The most likely understanding of the significance of the number of fish caught is the reference to fish in Ezekiel 47.[75] If we consider that Jesus said to his disciples that if they followed him, he would send them out to fish for people (Mt. 4:19), then this miraculous catch of fish could relate to seeking and saving the lost (Lk. 19:10).

Ezekiel 47 describes a river that flows eastward out of the temple, that will contain a large number of fish of many kinds wherever it flows. Along this river, there will be fishermen and there will be places from En Gedi to En Eglaim to spread their nets. According to the standard Hebrew practice of Gematria, the words 'En Eglaim' in numbers totals 153.[76]

It is therefore likely that the apostle John is linking this story in his gospel to that of Ezekiel 47 because John made extensive use of the imagery, structures, and themes of the prophecy of Ezekiel. Jesus' gospel is to go to all nations of the world, people from every tribe and language (aka many kinds of fish) will be there before Jesus' throne (Rev. 7:9).

---

[75] Theologians differ in their view on what 153 represents
[76] Gematria is the practice of assigning a numerical value to a name, word or phrase by reading it as a number, or sometimes by using an alphanumerical cipher

So Jesus is reminding Peter of his role in the great commission, he wasn't just wanting to resolve his feelings of failure. Peter's restoration was to lead to the gospel reaching more people. Peter was not to shrink back but to take seriously what it means to follow Jesus, by continuing to demonstrate the nearness of the kingdom of God to people (Mt. 10:7).

If disappointment and discouragement are left unchecked, the danger is that we will stop following Jesus and our efforts to save the lost and disciple other Christians could diminish.

An invitation from Jesus

Have you made a promise to Jesus that, like Peter, you meant it when you said it, but you have not managed to keep it? Maybe you've made promises about how you might treat your spouse and children, but you haven't always managed to do that and it's created a sense of failure in you.

Maybe you've made promises when you've had a powerful encounter with God, and you said things like "I'm never going to let go of you", "I'm always going to pursue you in every circumstance" or "I've seen enough miracles I'm never going to stop praying for them". Yet somehow troublesome circumstances have come along and you have withdrawn from God.

When I (Mark) entered the Church of St Peter in Gallicantu, I felt an invitation to sit with Jesus. I sat down and Jesus began to speak with me about the times I felt I had failed him. His love, like a bloodhound, began to search out in my conscious and subconscious every moment when I felt I had failed Jesus throughout my life.

As his love found each of these places, they melted away every sense of failure and disappointment in myself. These moments went back over decades and I realised I had been carrying a sense of failure for many years. It was a truly profound healing experience and one I will never forget.

I realised that the encounter Peter had with Jesus to restore him was available to each one of us. Peter's story in the Bible was not there just for him, it has been available for every Christian for the last two thousand years. Jesus does not want any of us to become stuck due to any unresolved internal clutter.

If we want more of God in our lives then we will need to respond to Jesus' invitation to resolve any lingering failure or disappointment. If you have broken a promise that you made to God, Jesus wants to restore you as he did Peter. His love is more powerful than any failure, discouragement and disappointment.

You may feel unworthy or beyond redemption, but such feelings are misleading. God is fully aware of how you feel and why you feel that way. His love can penetrate your deepest wounds and emotions; nothing is impossible for him (Lk. 1:37). Like Peter, Jesus invites you into a conversation with him.

Will we make space for Jesus by dealing with any unresolved discouragement?

Reflection

Consider these verses:

> I have chosen you and have not rejected you. So do not fear, for I am with you; do not be dismayed, for I am your God. I will strengthen you and help you; I will uphold you with my righteous right hand.
>
> Isaiah 41:9-10

> May the God of hope fill you with all joy and peace as you trust in him, so that you may overflow with hope by the power of the Holy Spirit.
>
> Romans 15:13

Ask Father God:

- Lord, is there anything that I am disappointed or discouraged about?
- Lord, have I stopped following you and got stuck in any way?
- Lord, do I feel that I have failed or disappointed you in any way?

Prayer:

Thank you Father God that you are gracious and compassionate. I turn my heart fully towards you and choose to love you as you meet me in any struggles or hindrances I am experiencing. I will follow you during the good and bad times.

To do:

- Consider the reasons why you may have withdrawn from God due to discouragement, failure or disappointment.
- Assess any reasons as to whether they are Biblical, fair, reasonable or true. Pray through them, asking Father God for his perspective.
- If you are stuck in your journey, make practical steps to move forward based on your love for God, such as talking to someone about it.

Further reading:

- Psalm 34:17-19
- Romans 8:26-30
- 2 Corinthians 4:16-18

KNOW YOU ARE WONDERFULLY MADE

It is an absolute human certainty that no one can know his own beauty or perceive a sense of his own worth until it has been reflected back to him in the mirror of another loving, caring human being.
(John Joseph Powell, Author)

"Jesus came into the room, pointed over at me, and spoke ... then everything changed"

During my teenage years, I (Fiona) had a self-destruct mechanism that was often at work in my mind, like a self-sabotage process. This would look like driving along in the car on the motorway and be feeling completely fine and okay, but then I would have an overwhelming urge that I should just drive my car into the central reservation at high speed.

Another example was whilst I was travelling to France. I was on a ferry, looking forward to the journey and feeling excited about having a day trip, but then just having an overwhelming urge to throw myself over the side of the ferry. I often wondered where on earth such thoughts came from, as they were a regular feature, even when I wasn't feeling like I was struggling mentally or emotionally or feeling in a dark place.

On days when I was in a place of particularly struggling and feeling very down, my mind would often go to the place where I would think about ending my own life. I would think about where, when, and how to end my life. It became an unhealthy preoccupation when I was at a low point in life.

When I became a Christian at 19, those thoughts were still there but less frequent. When they came along I would more often question where did that come from? I would wonder what the source of those thoughts was and why was I having them. Whereas before I was a Christian, I would think about it and get taken down a kind of dark thought path.

In my mid-twenties, I went to a conference and I remember it was packed with people and there was standing room only. There was a very powerful sung worship time and I was lying on the floor and I had an encounter with God. I was curled up in a little ball, and it felt like I was a foetus.

Maybe this was what the Bible describes as a vision ... in my mind I saw my Mum and Dad were sitting in the doctor's consultation room at our local GP practice and I was in my mum's womb. There was a big oak desk in front of us and our family GP on the other side of it. The GP leaned across the desk to my mum and said, "I recommend to you that you have a termination because your health, and possibly your life, is at risk if you continue with this pregnancy".

My mum had told me that when she was pregnant with me, she had a very serious infection which needed an operation because antibiotics would not have resolved it. I knew that she had been offered to terminate the pregnancy to remove the potential risk to her own life.

Whilst I was in this encounter moment, I thought this was unusual. I was not sure why I was thinking about and experiencing this discussion. Then at that moment, the door of the GPs room burst open and Jesus came into the room, pointed over at me, and spoke. He said, "She shall live!"

Then everything changed.

From that time on, the desire to end my own life stopped; it wasn't an issue anymore. It seemed like there was a spiritual root to it. It was like that somebody had spoken death over me even before I was born. I don't know how the dynamic of that works, but the issue was there and then it wasn't, because Jesus spoke *life* over me.

That encounter changed everything! Many years later I started working with young people who struggle with self-harm, and feeling suicidal, some of whom have attempted suicide. They are often in a very dark and difficult place in terms of their thinking, their emotions and their mental health. It is incredible how God changed my life and transformed me to a place where I am working with those in a place where I once was.

A global issue

The World Health Organisation (WHO) reported in 2019 that more than 700,000 died by suicide and that for each suicide, there were likely more than twenty suicide attempts. [77] Globally, suicide occurs in all regions of the world and equates to one in every hundred deaths. Suicide is the fourth leading cause of death in 15-29 year-olds.

There are multiple reasons for suicide, but suicide often happens impulsively in moments of crisis. WHO states risk factors include experiencing loss, loneliness, discrimination, a

---

[77] World Health Organisation. "Suicide prevention". *World Health Organisation.* https://www.who.int/health-topics/suicide#tab_tab_1

relationship break-up, financial problems, chronic pain and illness, violence, abuse, and humanitarian emergencies.

An additional suicide risk is self-hatred or self-loathing. One study shows that social media networking could normalise the risks of self-harm and suicidal ideation. [78] The posts analysed showed common themes of self-loathing (15%), feeling unloved (15%), self-harm (15%) and suicide (14%).

The tragic story of Molly Russell in 2017 demonstrated the effect of social media on her suicide.[79] The coroner concluded that it was not right to say Molly died by suicide because posts on Instagram and Pinterest had contributed to her death. He said, "She died from an act of self-harm while suffering from depression and the negative effects of online content."

In 2021, the NSPCC counselling service Childline received 24,200 calls about suicidal thoughts or feelings.[80] That averages a call every 21 minutes throughout the entire year. Molly's story was one of many tragedies that led to the UK's Online Safety Act 2023, which aims to keep children safe online. [81]

Self-loathing means you strongly dislike yourself.[82] It can lead to hating yourself and thinking that you are the worst person on the planet.[83] You can turn yourself into your own enemy and can have feelings of rage and disgust towards yourself. Worst of

---

[78] Cavazos-Rehg, Patricia. "An Analysis of Depression, Self-Harm, and Suicidal Ideation Content on Tumblr". *NCBI.* https://pubmed.ncbi.nlm.nih.gov/27445014
[79] Meaker, Morgan. "How A British Teen's Death Changed Social Media". *Wired.* https://www.wired.co.uk/article/how-a-british-teens-death-changed-social-media
[80] *NSPCC.* https://www.nspcc.org.uk
[81] UK Parliament. "Online Safety Act 2023". *Parliamentary Bills.* https://bills.parliament.uk/bills/3137
[82] Cambridge Dictionary. dictionary.cambridge.org/dictionary/english/self-loathing
[83] Woolfe, Sam. "The Connection Between Self-Hatred and Suicide". *HealthyPlace.* https://www.healthyplace.com/blogs/buildingselfesteem/2018/9/the-connection-between-self-hatred-and-suicide

all, it can lead you to believe you have no value and are not lovable.

Self-loathing can be defined as a constant belief or feeling of worthlessness, failure, inadequacy, and incompetence.[84] People feel they are not good enough and are undeserving of anything good in life. It can lead to self-punishment, isolation, anxiety, depression and self-harm.

Common causes of self-loathing are childhood trauma, abuse, violence, low self-esteem, a poor family environment, bullying, comparisons of oneself and others, unrealistic high expectations of oneself, extreme self-criticism, feeling out of place, and the inability to let go of past mistakes. The ultimate destination of self-loathing is self-hatred.[85]

How do we define our self-worth?

If we don't discover our self-worth and learn to love ourselves it will most likely create significant internal clutter in our lives that will hinder us from loving ourselves, God, and others. Seeing ourselves as God sees us enables us to truly understand our value, worth and identity.

King David understood that his self-worth came from God:

> For you created my inmost being; you knit me together in my mother's womb.
>
> I praise you because I am fearfully and wonderfully made; your works are wonderful, I know that full well.

---

[84] Tee-Melegrito, Rachel. "What to know about self-loathing". *Medical News Today.* https://www.medicalnewstoday.com/articles/self-loathing
[85] Mental Health America. "I hate myself". *Mental Health America.* https://screening.mhanational.org/content/i-hate-myself

> My frame was not hidden from you when I was made in the secret place, when I was woven together in the depths of the earth.
>
> Your eyes saw my unformed body; all the days ordained for me were written in your book before one of them came to be. How precious to me are your thoughts, God! How vast is the sum of them!
>
> Psalm 139:13-17

When King David described himself as 'wonderfully made' he based that on God's works being wonderful. God is the creator, so this is his objective view of who we are (Isa. 45:12). This is not based on our effort, performance, a subjective feeling, or whim – it is based on the perspective of an infallible God.

If we have a different view of ourselves, which has been shaped by other perspectives and experiences, then we need to go through a process of aligning our thoughts and emotions of ourselves with what God thinks and feels about us. This can be done by studying the Bible, prayer, self-compassion, self-care, encouragement of others and maybe also some therapy.

We will need to challenge and reframe our thoughts, which can begin by asking questions of ourselves. We can ask why we hate ourselves, who told us that and where did I learn that? Understanding the root of why you may hate yourself and what triggers it is often the beginning of the journey to overcome it.

This is likely to require you to forgive yourself. Jesus asks us to forgive others when they sin against us, but that also applies to ourselves. When we hate or loathe ourselves, it is as though we are sinning against ourselves because we don't treat ourselves in the way God does. Forgiving ourselves when we get it wrong or think badly about ourselves is self-loving.

Forgiving ourselves will undermine any internal self-criticism, it will empower you to overcome the need to be perfect. This will help you accept the parts of your life you don't like, rather than hating them. Forgiveness will also free you from difficult emotions that may have been locked up for some time.

The apostle Paul describes how husbands and wives should love each other, he contrasts loving others with self-love:

> Husbands, love your wives, just as Christ loved the church and gave himself up for her to make her holy, cleansing her by the washing with water through the word, and to present her to himself as a radiant church, without stain or wrinkle or any other blemish, but holy and blameless.
>
> In this same way, husbands ought to love their wives as their own bodies. He who loves his wife loves himself. After all, no one ever hated their own body, but they feed and care for their body, just as Christ does the church – for we are members of his body.
>
> 'For this reason a man will leave his father and mother and be united to his wife, and the two will become one flesh.' This is a profound mystery – but I am talking about Christ and the church. However, each one of you also must love his wife as he loves himself, and the wife must respect her husband.
>
> Ephesians 5:25-33

Loving ourselves and loving others is connected. If we don't love ourselves we may find it difficult to love, trust and be vulnerable with those that love us. The apostle Paul uses the standard for the husband of loving his body and self, as how he should love his wife. When we learn to love ourselves, it becomes easier to love others.

"Love" in this passage means to welcome, to be fond of, to love dearly, to be well pleased and contented.[86] It is the same word that is used to describe how God loves the world (Jn. 3:16). It is the highest form of love in the Greek language and is often described as a self-sacrificial love.[87]

This is how we should love ourselves and others. The apostle Paul also makes the statement "no one ever hated their own body, but they feed and care for their body" (Eph. 5:29). The Biblical norm is that we love ourselves, so any other perspective does not align with God's blueprint for our lives.

If we love ourselves, we will be patient and kind to ourselves, and we won't compare our value to others. We will treat ourselves with humility, we will not have a poor opinion of ourselves, we will not be angry with ourselves or keep a record of the things we get wrong. Our love for ourselves will be based upon truth and we will protect, trust, and hope in ourselves. We will not give up on ourselves (1 Cor. 13:4-8).

This is how God loves us and is therefore how we should love ourselves. King Solomon says, "For as he thinks within himself, so he is." (Prv. 23:7). How we think about ourselves directly influences whether we consider ourselves valuable and loveable. It can also affect the value and love for others.

---

[86] agapaō. Strong's G25
[87] There are four Greek words used to describe love: Eros, Phileo, Agape and Storge.

The author and therapist Shannon L. Alder said, "The way you think about yourself determines your reality." We have a choice of how we define the reality of our internal world – a good start would be by loving ourselves.

He chose us

When others communicate our value to us it can touch us deeply, give us a positive sense of self and encourage us. More importantly, it affects our self-esteem, which is the belief and confidence in our own ability and value.[88] Another way of describing it is self-worth – which is defined as "the internal sense of being good enough and worthy of love and belonging from others."[89]

Jesus says to his disciples "You did not choose me, but I chose you" (Jn. 15:16). The fact that God chose us means we have immense value and worth. Not only are we chosen, but we have been seated with Jesus in heavenly realms "in order that in the coming ages he might show the incomparable riches of his grace" (Eph. 2:7) – that is truly profound!

This communicates to us that we have great worth to God. God has not just taken notice of you or just taken interest in you, but he has chosen you to be an object of his love for eternity (Deut. 10:15). God's love for us defines our true self-worth, not other's words or actions toward us. Seeing ourselves from God's perspective is the only way we can understand our true worth.

We may define ourselves by what we do, what job we have, how much money we have, our personal achievements, how we look and dress, and other people's opinions. We can also go out

---

[88] Cambridge Dictionary. https://dictionary.cambridge.org/dictionary/english/self-esteem
[89] UNCW. "Self-Worth". *UNCW.* https://uncw.edu/seahawk-life/health-wellness/counseling/self-help-resources/self-worth

of our way to seek approval from authority figures in our lives. These can be helpful, but the trouble with them is that they are often conditional.

If affirmation is only given to us by authority figures based on our performance, it can create a set of values and behaviours that communicate value through what we do. If we have a bad day or fail to meet someone's expectations of us, our value may be diminished. Self-worth can then be built around pleasing others.

The apostle John tells us that God *is* love:

> Dear friends, let us love one another, for love comes from God. Everyone who loves has been born of God and knows God. Whoever does not love does not know God, because God is love.
>
> This is how God showed his love among us: he sent his one and only Son into the world that we might live through him. This is love: not that we loved God, but that he loved us and sent his Son as an atoning sacrifice for our sins.
>
> Dear friends, since God so loved us, we also ought to love one another. No one has ever seen God; but if we love one another, God lives in us and his love is made complete in us ... And so we know and rely on the love God has for us.
>
> God is love. Whoever lives in love lives in God, and God in them. This is how love is made complete among us so that we will have confidence on the day of judgment: in this world we are like Jesus. There is no fear in love. But perfect love drives out fear, because

> fear has to do with punishment. The one who fears is not made perfect in love.
>
> 1 John 4:7-12 & 16-18

Love is best understood when we experience God's love (Rom. 5:5). His experience of love defines who we are and who we belong to. It shows us what love is, how to receive it and how to give it. Experiencing God's love can powerfully affect our self-worth. It shows us who we are and whose we are.

When we become a Christian, we can leave behind any experiences that taught us we had little self-worth. We can embrace God's perspective about us, leaving behind fear – fear of rejection, fear of abandonment, fear of not being accepted, fear of being punished and fear of not being enough.

Brené Brown has spent two decades studying courage, vulnerability, shame, and empathy. She writes in her book The Gifts of Imperfection:

> Wholehearted living is about engaging with our lives from a place of worthiness.
>
> It means cultivating the courage, compassion and connection to wake up in the morning and think, 'No matter what gets done and how much is left undone, I am enough.'
>
> It's going to bed at night thinking, 'Yes, I am imperfect and vulnerable and sometimes afraid, but that doesn't change the truth that I am also brave and worthy of love and belonging.

Because we are made in the image of God, we are worthy of love, we are enough in who God made us (Gen. 1:27). We don't need to perform or meet other expectations to be accepted and know we are loved. As children of God, we have an eternal relationship with God and belong to him (Rom. 14:8).

God "chose us in him before the creation of the world to be holy and blameless in his sight. In love he predestined us for adoption to sonship through Jesus Christ, in accordance with his pleasure and will." (Eph. 1:4-5). God's love and his adoption define our self-worth, value, meaning and purpose.

Helping others

In 2020 I (Fiona) started working in a job providing support to young people in hospital because of their self-harm or suicidal feelings. Due to COVID-19 lockdowns in the UK, we initially provided support via phone for referrals before providing support directly within the hospital A&E department.

On meeting a young person in a hospital, they were usually in a bad place, saying that their life wasn't working, they felt overwhelmed, and may have also felt like it was never going to change. In these moments we would look to bring hope to them, saying just because it felt bleak at that time, to not assume that it was always going to continue to be that way.

Because of my own story, I would say to them it can change and ask them about their dreams and passions. Then talk with them about what is in their heart, and what they want to do with their life and affirm the strengths I could see in them. I sought to bring them hope so that their situation could change and wouldn't always be what it felt like in that moment.

When I was living inside my head struggling with similar thoughts, I didn't want to talk to my family about it because I didn't want to hurt them. I didn't want to talk to my friends about it in case they completely freaked out. As a Christian, you are unlikely to talk about it because it can sound quite shocking to even say things like that.

Culturally, it's still very taboo to talk about feeling suicidal and there's still lots of stigma around it and we rarely talk about this stuff. There is also a real fear that when you do talk about it, people may get scared or give an unhelpful response, saying you just need to do this or that. Giving a response that is dismissive or superficial and won't address what you're struggling with and can be quite unhelpful.

During these difficult moments, people can internalise a perspective that life will never get better or that they are worthless. They can get entrenched in that way of thinking and go around the same loop with the same thoughts the whole time. When we are in this situation, we may need someone else to help us see that.

When someone is struggling with thoughts of self-harm, they can feel quite overwhelmed and in emotional pain. It can be difficult for them to see past their struggle and immediate future. It also may have been their norm for a long time. If this is the case there are usually no quick fixes, but rather will require someone to walk with them on a journey to recovery.

I was a Christian for years before the encounter with Jesus I described earlier, and in that moment everything didn't get fixed. I still had to do all sorts of journeying around addressing my low self-esteem, my low self-worth, my negative view of myself, and who I was. I needed to create a new stronger norm for my self-worth in my thoughts and emotions.

Without resolving these, suicidal thoughts can play into feelings of worthlessness, feeling like if they no longer existed the world wouldn't even notice; what's the point of carrying on because it's just too hard? The struggle can be so exhausting and so mentally and emotionally taxing. Sometimes they may reach a point of feeling like they just can't carry on anymore.

Those who are in this situation don't just need empathy, prayer and encouragement – they also require getting people who are skilled in understanding where these thoughts and emotions come from. They need help to recognise the unhelpful, negative and untrue things they are hearing and to replace them with the truth.

To get well requires them to believe, rehearse, immerse and live in the reality of truths. This is a process and will likely include times when they feel they are going down negative thought patterns in their mind and emotions. They will need to learn to push back on these negative thoughts that come to kill, steal and destroy (Jn. 10:10).

Think about the process of pulling up established weeds and replacing them with plants and flowers. Firstly, it requires the weeds and roots to be pulled out – think of these as the lies around self-worth and suicidal thoughts. Weeds choke what grows in soil, so these need to come out first.

Secondly, the soil needs to be a place that is full of nutrients – think of this as a person's support that will walk with them to freedom. Family, friends, volunteers and professionals who encourage them to believe that life can be different and that they have a different future will create soil where new truths can grow.

Thirdly, new plants and flowers are required – think about these as the truths that can change how people think. New truths are required to replace unhelpful and negative thoughts. Instead, these new truths can bring a person thoughts of peace, hope, safety, belonging and knowing they are loved.

Fourthly, the plants and flowers need to be established within their new soil. For plants and trees, this process may take some time. Think about this as a good environment in which to learn how to live free. This will be an environment that will build up and support, tending to the new plants to ensure they grow strong.

Knowing you are loved

Self-loathing is internal clutter that can be a significant hindrance to experiencing more of God in our lives. When someone tells us that we are loved by God, our internal world can cause us to reject that truth. We may know that truth as a logical statement or say we believe it is true in our minds, but it may not penetrate our hearts if we have rejected ourselves.

God wants us to know we are fearfully and wonderfully made. None of us is a mistake, none of us is unlovable, and all of us are treasured by him. If experiences in your life have left you feeling rejected and unloved, then it is time to discover the truth about yourself. God's truth can overturn any negative experiences you have had (Jn. 8:31-32).

For most, the journey will start with being open and honest with people they trust. This journey will most likely involve encounters with Jesus' love, renewing our minds on Biblical truths, forgiveness, prayer, and maybe counselling or therapy. We do not need to settle with a viewpoint that we are rejected, but instead, embrace the truth that we are loved with an everlasting love.

If this is you, why not start this journey now? Or, why not ask Jesus to help you understand what is stopping you? There is nothing in the universe that can separate you from the love of God. He is more able and willing than you think to deal with whatever may have caused you to hate yourself.

Will we make space for Jesus by dealing with any unresolved self-loathing?

Reflection

Consider these verses:

> *From one man he made all the nations, that they should inhabit the whole earth; and he marked out their appointed times in history and the boundaries of their lands. God did this so that they would seek him and perhaps reach out for him and find him, though he is not far from any one of us.*
>
> Acts 17:26-27

> *In all these things we are more than conquerors through him who loved us. For I am convinced that neither death nor life, neither angels nor demons, neither the present nor the future, nor any powers, neither height nor depth, nor anything else in all creation, will be able to separate us from the love of God that is in Christ Jesus our Lord.*
>
> Romans 8:37-39

Ask Father God:

- Lord, have I believed any lies about my self-worth? Father God, what do you value and love about me?
- Lord, where have the emotional wounds I have sustained come from?
- Lord, is there anything that I need to forgive others or myself for?

- Lord, how can I understand and experience more of your love?

Prayer:

Thank you Father God that you have always loved me. Help me to see myself as you see me. Thank you that you chose when I would be born so that I could seek you and find you. Thank you that I am your design and that you created me to experience your love. Please remove any internal clutter in my life that hinders me from experiencing your love.

To do:

- Make a list of reasons why you are loved and find evidence by considering relevant Bible verses and positive feedback that others have given you.
- Make a list of three things that you like about yourself and practice self-compassion by encouraging and celebrating yourself.

Further reading:

- Romans 12:1-2
- Genesis 1:26-27 & 31
- 2 Corinthians 5:16-17

BE PATIENT IN AFFLICTION

Out of suffering have emerged the strongest souls; the most massive characters are seared with scars.
(Khalil Gibran, Author)

"I'm gonna be a history maker in this land."

During our twenties, we regularly went to concerts by a band called Delirious?. We were impressed by how they integrated worship into their gigs and had a greater focus on Jesus and their audience than on themselves. As we sang, we encountered the tangible presence of God.

Their songs inspired us to live 'all out' for God and increased our passion to serve him. Their song *History Makers* seemed to capture our dedication to Jesus, to do whatever he asked, whatever the cost. We believed anything was possible and that changing the world was within our reach.

Yet we found that life was not as straightforward as we thought it would be. Over the next twenty-five years, we experienced the untimely death of loved ones, being overlooked, disappointment, discouragement, disinheritance, false accusations, frustration, stress, anxiety, trauma, and illness. At times the journey was tough.

Jesus said to his disciples they would have trouble in this world (Jn. 16:33). But, when trouble came, our beliefs in God at the time struggled to incorporate our suffering. We had to learn to face trouble head-on and find God in the journey to recovery. This was easier said than done.

Suffering is rarely clutter that we can throw out of our lives, rather the clutter amid suffering is the unhelpful way that we can respond to it. Jesus concluded his words to his disciples during the Passover Festival by saying "All this I have told you so that you will not fall away" (Jn. 16:1). How we choose to respond to suffering can influence whether we may or may not stop following Jesus.

Experiencing physical illness or mental trauma can be extremely hard to bear. The Centre for Addiction and Mental Health says "Experiencing a traumatic event can harm a person's sense of safety, sense of self, and ability to regulate emotions and navigate relationships. Long after the traumatic event occurs, people with trauma can often feel shame, helplessness, powerlessness and intense fear."[90]

When we suffer, we are likely to ask: "Where are you God?", "Why do I have to suffer?" and "Will God take my suffering away?". These are important questions, but perhaps other questions could be "Can I find God in my suffering?" and "Can I be patient in my suffering?" or maybe, more importantly, asking ourselves "What can I learn from how Jesus suffered?".

Experiencing suffering requires us to navigate troubled waters like no other challenge. It will test our resolve and our faith. The temptation will most likely come for us to give up on, blame or be angry with God. Yet the journey of suffering can include some of the most profound moments of our lives. So is there a way to navigate such troubled waters?

---

[90] CAMH. "Trauma". *The Centre for Addiction and Mental Health.* http://www.camh.ca

What we didn't know when we were singing *History Makers* in our twenties was that there was a backstory of suffering. Martin Smith (Delirious? lead vocalist), his wife Anna and Jon Thatcher (Delirious? bass guitar) were involved in a car accident in 1995. Jon and Anna were physically unharmed, but Martin was hospitalised for several weeks with broken bones.

While in the hospital Martin Smith suffered depression before deciding to become a full-time musician. The band then changed its name in January 1996 and began working on a new album, which included the song '*History Makers*'. This led to them becoming one of the most popular Christian bands in the UK and United States.

It matters how we respond to suffering because it can influence our future. Elisabeth Kubler-Ross, who is best known for the Five Stages of Grief model, said "The most beautiful people we have known are those who have known defeat, known suffering, known struggle, known loss, and have found their way out of those depths."

Why me?

In my (Mark) early fifties the issue of suffering came to a head when I was diagnosed with PTSD.[91] An event in my life triggered traumatic experiences from both my childhood and adulthood. In parallel, I was also diagnosed with two other health issues. The combined impact of this meant I hit rock bottom. This also led to Fiona experiencing significant stress.

I was completely overwhelmed emotionally, experiencing fear, hopelessness, and anxiety. I felt I lost a significant part of my

---

[91] NHS. "Overview - Post-traumatic stress disorder". *NHS*. https://www.nhs.uk/mental-health/conditions/post-traumatic-stress-disorder-ptsd/overview

brain capacity. For months I slept for 10-12 hours a night and during the day stared blankly at the wall and sat crying. My confidence in God's goodness was repeatedly questioned.

The dual challenge of dealing with the trauma and not understanding why I had to suffer was overwhelming. I questioned God's love for me, whether he cared about my situation and if he was even willing to heal me. I needed help because at this point the answers, if there were any, seemed beyond my reach and understanding.

Situations like this test our resilience and reveal what we really put our trust in. There is nowhere to hide when multiple tough questions arise, and we have a choice to either engage with them or avoid them. It did not take me long to feel sorry for myself and ask, "Why me?"

Whilst this is an understandable question, it is a self-centred perspective and is therefore unlikely to provide any helpful answers. The reality is that everyone suffers, it is part of being in a world broken by sin. When we realise that we are not alone, we can empathise and learn from others who have suffered.

My journey of recovery began with Cognitive Behavioural Therapy (CBT).[92] CBT is a talking therapy that can help you manage your issues by changing the way you think and behave. After twelve months of therapy, I was feeling almost back to normal, but it was a new normal, one that could incorporate my experiences of trauma.

---

[92] NHS. "Overview - Cognitive behavioural therapy (CBT)". *NHS*. https://www.nhs.uk/mental-health/talking-therapies-medicine-treatments/talking-therapies-and-counselling/cognitive-behavioural-therapy-cbt/overview/

During this time, I also needed to update my beliefs in God which allowed for suffering to be part of my Christian journey.[93] For me, this meant I had to define in more detail what I meant by saying 'God is good'. I thought that his goodness would protect me from harm, and I struggled to understand when it didn't.

Our core beliefs are more complex than simple statements of faith. Within a core belief, we define expectations about God, ourselves, other people and the world in general. These expectations then shape our thinking about how life should work. These may differ based upon situation and context. For example, we may then expect God to protect us and keep us safe from all harm.

These core beliefs can be shaped by our upbringing, authority figures, friends, culture, religion, and life experiences (both positive and negative). When we experience trauma these core beliefs are likely to be challenged, making the journey of suffering harder to navigate. If this is the case, we will need to create time to assess and update our beliefs.

The apostle Paul instructs us to renew our minds so our thinking aligns with God's perspective. The apostle Paul says that this will be transformational and we will be "able to test and approve what God's will is – his good, pleasing and perfect will." (Rom. 12:2). In every circumstance it is important to know his will, including when we are suffering.

I had to examine what I meant by my belief that 'God is good' by listing all the implications associated with that belief. I then went back to the Bible and read verses about suffering to see

---

[93] Mark found the tool *Old System New System* helpful to update my core beliefs. You can find a free worksheet here: https://www.getselfhelp.co.uk/docs/OldSystemNewSystem.pdf

what they said, with the aim of understanding God's perspective. This allowed me to update this core belief, so it could incorporate experiencing suffering.

This was a difficult exercise to do because the new core belief would mean that I had to allow for potentially suffering again in the future. My new core belief was still centred on 'God is good' but was updated to say that his goodness doesn't promise to protect me from all harm, but when I do suffer, he will be with me always.

It may sound counterintuitive but accepting that suffering is part of life provides more robust and flexible core beliefs.[94] It means I have more confidence to navigate suffering should it come again. I have learnt some valuable lessons about God, myself, and my faith. One of the most important lessons to learn was to ask for help and not suffer in silence.

Freefalling

One of the most adventurous things I (Mark) have ever done is freefalling at 125mph when I did a tandem skydive to raise money for the charity that Fiona works for. You board a plane strapped to a professional skydiver, climb to 15,000 feet, and jump out the door of an aeroplane!

Two of my sons joined me and one of them jumped before me. To see my son drop like a stone out of an aeroplane door before my eyes was quite an experience, especially when it was my turn next! So, with my adrenaline pumping, part of me wanted to jump and another part did not.

---

[94] For a detailed analysis of suffering, we would recommend the book: Lewis, C.S. *The Problem of Pain*. The Centenary Press, 1940.

As the professional skydiver and I jumped, we somersaulted in the air a couple of times and started to fall at 125mph. I wish I could say it was a pleasant experience but I felt disoriented and sick. I was also looking straight down and could feel myself falling straight at it. The noise of the air rushing past my ears was deafening.

I was freefalling for about sixty seconds which felt like a lifetime. About halfway through I started to get hold of my emotions and engage with the moment. Despite my feelings, I wanted to remember this once in a lifetime experience. As I engaged, I started to look around and see the amazing view and feel the rush of air going past my body.

As I started to acclimatise and orientate myself to this moment, the professional skydiver opened the parachute and suddenly I felt caught up in a mid-air emergency brake. I was then struck by the absolute quiet as I gracefully glided down through the air. I had time to think, look, breathe, and make the most of this experience.

When I was diagnosed with PTSD, I went into free fall emotionally and spiritually. I felt overwhelmed, hopeless, and lost. The deafening noise inside my head was hard to bear, the fountain of never-ending tears was exhausting. I did not feel in control of my feelings. I would frequently say to God "This journey is too hard, I don't think I can make it, please take this from me".

It was only when I started therapy during this free falling that I started to engage my thoughts and feelings. My therapist validated my experience and affirmed that my thoughts and feelings were normal for someone who has experienced trauma. A small glimmer of hope came that maybe, possibly, there was a way to navigate through this.

The glimmer of hope was like the parachute opening, even though it didn't feel as dramatic as the skydive. I was no longer freefalling and had the support of therapy, my wife and praying friends. Just like the slow descent when using a parachute, I started a slow journey of healing, which was at times frustratingly slow.

When doing a skydive, the parachute opens, and you are hanging mid-air until you reach the ground. This is what the healing journey often felt like for me, I was trapped in a very slow process without knowing how long it would take. I did however choose to look around and evaluate the view of life from the perspective of suffering.

A much-needed compass

As I contemplated suffering, I decided I needed to better engage with Father God. Simply blaming him for not removing me from this difficult journey was just creating distance between us. This started a very tentative exploration of what the Bible said about suffering. I realised I had a choice to engage with the process, resent it or fight it.

For my faith in God to survive I knew I needed a compass to navigate the suffering I was experiencing. I knew I had two main challenges – could I be patient and find God's comfort during suffering? I started with this verse "Be joyful in hope, patient in affliction, faithful in prayer." (Rom. 12:12).

My patience had a limit but now needed to grow beyond it to deal with suffering. As with any personal growth, this needed encouragement from loved ones and friends. Several friends rallied and made time for me, offering a regular coffee or a walk to listen and help. The recovery journey is not one to do alone.

Along with PTSD, I needed to address some other health conditions I had. This required various medical examinations, which triggered traumatic childhood memories of invasive and painful medical procedures. This was extremely tough to deal with because I needed to go through the examinations and procedures to enable the doctors to diagnose my physical health conditions.

Being resourceful, Fiona contacted about thirty Christian friends to pray for me, and this made a real difference. I needed an MRI scan and because of the PTSD, the thought of this caused havoc with my emotions. On the day of the appointment, I woke up feeling able to go through with having the scan. I knew this was because people were praying.

This group of friends continued to pray throughout my recovery journey, and I don't think I would have made it without them. Do not suffer alone, find those who will support you, and do not be embarrassed to ask. I have been continually amazed at those who *wanted to help*, suffering provides people the opportunity to demonstrate love.

One of the most well-known Bible passages is Psalm 23:

> The Lord is my shepherd, I lack nothing.
>
> He makes me lie down in green pastures, he leads me beside quiet waters, he refreshes my soul.
>
> He guides me along the right paths for his name's sake.
>
> Even though I walk through the darkest valley, I will fear no evil, for you are with me; your rod and your staff, they comfort me.

> You prepare a table before me in the presence of my enemies.
>
> You anoint my head with oil; my cup overflows. Surely your goodness and love will follow me all the days of my life, and I will dwell in the house of the Lord for ever.

If there is ever a moment when we want these verses to be personally real, it is when we suffer. Yet in our instant Western society, we may have expectations of this Psalm that are not included within these verses. God's promise in this Psalm is to comfort us, but it will be done in the way he chooses.

The word "comfort" used in Psalm 23 means to comfort, have compassion, be sorry and console, in other words, to alleviate the grief, sense of loss, or trouble.[95] This is God's heart to us when we suffer, his desire and intent is to comfort us when we are struggling. We can therefore seek and find the comfort that God makes available to us.

For me, the challenge was about how to receive God's comfort, not about his ability to provide it. One of the impacts of PTSD on me was that my self-worth hit a low and the value I had for myself diminished significantly. I could not operate like I usually did and therefore felt I offered little value to my family and friends. I regularly felt like a failure.

I did not feel lovable and had to learn to love myself in my suffering. I had to rethink my sense of value and as I did, I began to experience God's comfort. Suffering can be a tutor to show us how we define ourselves and whether we value

---

[95] nāham, Strong's H5162

ourselves from God's perspective. As I learned to love myself in suffering it also meant I took better care of myself.

God's comfort came in different ways and at times in unexpected ways. When you are at a low point, a phone call or message from a concerned friend means a lot. Having someone who genuinely asks how you are and listens to your reply is life-giving. Words of affirmation, acts of service, receiving gifts, quality time and physical touch are ways to show love.[96]

It is important to note that within this Psalm the promise of comfort is in the context of Jesus being our shepherd. Middle Eastern shepherds are different to Western shepherds because the terrain is very different. In the West, shepherds look after their sheep in green fields, in the Middle East shepherds look after their sheep in sun-scorched lands.

In verse 2, the green pastures and water that are referred to are usually very small areas of water and food that only last the sheep a few hours. The sheep are totally dependent on *daily following* their shepherd on the right paths to stay alive. Receiving comfort from God requires us to follow Jesus day by day.

When we suffer, we may need to navigate one day at a time. The comfort we received from God yesterday may not be the same kind of comfort we need today. One day we may need hope, the next love, and the following day inspiration. We need to trust God in his ability to shepherd us day by day while we suffer. Letting God be our compass and guide is key because he knows us better than we know ourselves.

---

[96] Love Languages. "Relationships don't have to be complicated". *Love Languages.* https://5lovelanguages.com

Middle Eastern shepherds carried two key pieces of equipment, namely their rod and staff and both are used to bring comfort in Psalm 23.[97] The rod, an extension of the owner's right arm, is used to primarily defend the sheep. It is a symbol of his strength, power, and authority.

The rod is used to discipline wayward sheep that wandered away or came too close to danger. When we suffer, we can be vulnerable to wandering away from our faith and prone to seeking comfort in the wrong places. We can also be prone to believing things about God that are not true; for example, that he does not care about our suffering.

Part of God's comfort when we suffer is to protect us from harm. This will include protecting us from believing and doing wrong things, that could increase our suffering and impair our recovery. In these scenarios, the shepherd would throw the rod towards the sheep to encourage it back to the rest of the herd.

The rod was also used to examine the sheep, which is referred to in one of Ezekiel's prophecies (Ezk. 20:37). The sheep would come under the rod to be carefully examined for diseases and defects. We can be confident that when we suffer, God pays us careful attention and that he brings us closer under his rod to check on our welfare and wellbeing.

This is where the staff comes into play. The shepherd will use the staff to gather individual sheep to draw them close to himself for the examination. When we suffer there will be times when we feel far from God, but feelings can be misleading. God, the shepherd, will draw you close so he will be fully aware of your circumstances and internal world.

---

[97] Keller, Phillip. "Excerpts from: A Shepherd Looks At Psalm 23". *Antipas*. https://www.antipas.org/commentaries/articles/shepherd_psa23/shepherd_07.html

The staff is also used to guide sheep along new or difficult paths. The shepherd will use the staff to apply pressure to the side of the sheep to encourage it in the right direction. If a sheep gets stuck in a hole or brambles, the staff is used to lift them out of their predicament. The staff is our compass to navigate suffering.

During our journey through suffering, we will need to feel the pressure of God's comforting staff to keep us heading in the right direction. If we fall into a hole or get stuck in our pain, God will use his staff to lift us out and put us back on the path. We need to be patient with ourselves and let God's comfort keep us on track.

We need to guard against self-criticism, discouragement, and condemnation when we find the path difficult or lose our way. Suffering and trauma can be extremely difficult journeys and when at times we find it too much we need to remember that we have a shepherd who is "gracious and compassionate, slow to anger and rich in love." (Psalm 145:8).

Some of us may not recover from our suffering and end up with a disability or have an untimely death. These journeys are particularly tough for those who suffer, and for their family and friends. In these moments we need to find comfort that our life in this world is not the end and that God has a better eternal future for all those that love him.

His promise is this: "He will wipe every tear from their eyes. There will be no more death or mourning or crying or pain, for the old order of things has passed away." (Rev. 21:4). This is God's eternal future for us, where God will live among his people, and we will see his face (Rev. 22:4). Such a future hope can bring a different perspective to pain, suffering and injustice.

Walking alongside those who suffer

If you are walking alongside a loved one who is suffering, it will most likely cause you to suffer. Watching someone you love experiencing pain and struggling with their suffering can cause heartache. By definition, when you walk alongside them, you're hurting because they're hurting.

You may need to deal with your own sense of feeling helpless – you want to do something for them, but you don't always know what to do or how to do it. You may feel at the mercy of the process of what's going on, you may feel like you want to step in and do it for them, but you can't because they've got to go through it.

Another potential difficult dynamic is that initially, or at various points in the process, you might feel guilty because you thought you should have spotted the signs earlier. You may have thought they just needed to pray or change their lifestyle, missing the symptoms were pointing to something much deeper and more serious.

When walking alongside someone, you need to take care of yourself too. A useful analogy is the instructions given for a potential emergency on an aeroplane. When oxygen masks drop down on an aeroplane, you've got to put your own oxygen mask on before you can help anybody else with theirs. If you don't you could become a casualty yourself. You need to look after your own physical and mental health to avoid stress.

Having family and friends around you for support is key as it creates time for you to be able to talk about how it impacts you. Mental health still has, more than any other kind of health, a real stigma attached to it. This can also be true for many Christians. They may offer to cook a meal or pick the children up from school, but could be dismissive or not recognise how the suffering of a loved one is impacting you.

In the Bible, Job's friends were not much help to him when he struggled with his suffering. God rebuked them for not speaking the truth about him (Job 42:7). Christian friends may say in good faith that you just need to pray about it and tell you not to be anxious, and though this is likely to be well-meaning, it is not a substitute for providing the help you really need.

If your loved one had injured their leg, yes, we would pray that they get miraculously healed. But if they don't get healed, you would take them to hospital, so their leg could be treated. Our son had knee surgery following a torn ACL. A year later, he was still having physiotherapy. He went through a long, and at times, painful, healing process until he could run and play sports properly again.

The same is true with stress and mental illness, which also require a healing process over time. If your own mental health is impacted by walking beside a loved one, it can have a ripple effect on other areas of your life – family, work, friends etc. In this situation, reaching out to people for help is important. Isolation can often exacerbate things.

Take time to be with others to talk, to pray, to socialise and have some fun. This helps it not feel like your whole life is revolving around your loved one's suffering. It will also help you to find time to rest and recharge. Walking alongside those that suffer may be a long journey and requires ongoing stamina.

The value of just being able to go to somebody and offload and for somebody to just say, "Yes, that is a lot of stuff that you're coping with. I can see why that would be a struggle. I can see why you're finding it hard." Having somebody to validate that for you can be enough to make you think you are not going mad or struggling to cope in the midst of it all.

When people suffer trauma they are likely at times to struggle to manage their thoughts and emotions. In these situations, having a family member or friend who has the skills to be a co-regulator will be so helpful.[98] Co-regulators provide a calming presence and tone of voice, a safe environment, and the modelling of behaviours to help others manage their emotions.

Co-regulators don't panic when someone is having a difficult time with suffering. They communicate that they know how to cope with the situation and know what the person who is suffering needs. They are not dismissive with shallow statements such as "Just pull yourself together"; they offer insight and understanding.

If you are an individual who doesn't have those skills or feels completely at a loss as to how to walk alongside them, then get some help. Find someone who can help you understand what your loved one is experiencing and can coach you on how to co-regulate. This will also help you regulate your own emotions.

There are lots of online resources, phone apps and organisations that are available to provide help.[99] Don't let pride or thinking that mental issues are a sign of weakness get in the way of asking for help, just because you may be struggling to cope. Don't get caught up in worrying about what people may think. Getting help is the best thing you can do for yourself and your loved one who is suffering.

---

[98] Complex Trauma. "Co-regulation". *Complex Trauma Resources.* https://www.complextrauma.org/glossary/co-regulation
[99] For example, www.mentalhealth.org.uk/explore-mental-health/get-help, the moodtools.org app and www.camhs-resources.co.uk/websites

Suffering for doing good

Sometimes we suffer because we are persecuted for our faith. In 2018 it is estimated that 90,000 Christians were killed, which equates to one death every 6 minutes on average.[100] Christianity is the most persecuted religion; there were 360 million Christians in 2022 living in countries where persecution was significant.[101]

When Jesus opens the fifth seal in Revelation, the apostle John describes seeing those who have been martyred for their faith (Rev. 6:9-11). They are calling out in a loud voice for God to avenge their blood. Jesus encourages us not to be ashamed of him, but to deny ourselves and lose our life for him (Lk. 9:21-27).

Hebrews Chapter 11 is awe-inspiring. It is a list of men and women who stood firm in their faith in God, often in the midst of difficult circumstances. Some continued in faith despite not seeing the promises given to them by God occur in their lifetime. Some who are listed in this chapter *chose* to suffer.

The writer of Hebrews says of Moses that by faith he:

> "refused to be known as the son of Pharaoh's daughter. He chose to be ill-treated along with the people of God rather than to enjoy the fleeting pleasures of sin.

---

[100] Jones, Julie. "How many Christians are killed each year because of their faith?". *appgFoRB*. https://appgfreedomofreligionorbelief.org/how-many-christians-are-killed-each-year-because-of-their-faith

[101] Bandow, Doug. "Christianity Is the World's Most Persecuted Religion, Confirms New Report". *CATO Institute*. https://www.cato.org/commentary/christianity-worlds-most-persecuted-religion-confirms-new-report

> He regarded disgrace for the sake of Christ as of greater value than the treasures of Egypt, because he was looking ahead to his reward."
>
> Hebrews 11:24-26.

After describing the faith of many saints, the writer summarises as follows:

> "There were others who were tortured, refusing to be released so that they might gain an even better resurrection. Some faced jeers and flogging, and even chains and imprisonment. They were put to death by stoning; they were sawn in two; they were killed by the sword. They went about in sheepskins and goatskins, destitute, persecuted and ill-treated – the world was not worthy of them".
>
> Hebrews 11:35-38

When the apostle Paul writes about suffering, he describes fellowship, association, and joint participation:[102]

> "I want to know Christ – yes, to know the power of his resurrection and participation in his sufferings, becoming like him in his death, and so, somehow, attaining to the resurrection from the dead."
>
> Philippians 3:10-11.

For Paul and the heroes of faith listed in Hebrews 11, suffering was part of their journey. Not only did they choose to embrace it, but they understood *their response to it* was important to

---

[102] koinōnia, Strong's G2842

obtain a better eternal reward (1 Pet. 3:17). Jesus describes this reward in speaking to the church of Philadelphia, which is given to those who "Hold on to what you have, so that no one will take your crown." (Rev. 3:11).

The first disciples rejoiced that they were considered worthy of suffering disgrace for Jesus (Acts 5:40-41). For those who suffer for their faith, Jesus tells us there is a reward:

> "everyone who has left houses or brothers or sisters or father or mother or wife or children or fields for my sake will receive a hundred times as much and will inherit eternal life."

Matthew 19:29-30.

Timothy Cho, a North Korean human rights activist, said "What I can summarise is this, through twice escape and four times imprisonment – suffering does not destroy faith, but refines it. Sometimes I am grateful there was suffering I had gone through, because of that suffering, I am who I am today."[103]

Consider Jesus

When we are faced with suffering, we are encouraged to consider Jesus. He is our greatest motivation to persevere when we want to give up, when it gets too hard and when we feel overwhelmed. He is *the* example of someone who held fast to his relationship with the Father and fulfilled all that was asked of him, despite the opposition he faced

---

[103] Inspired Podcast. "Escape from North Korea". *Inspired Podcast.*
https://www.simonguillebaud.com/inspired-podcast

The writer of Hebrews gives us this encouragement:

> Therefore, since we are surrounded by such a great cloud of witnesses, let us throw off everything that hinders and the sin that so easily entangles.
>
> And let us run with perseverance the race marked out for us, fixing our eyes on Jesus, the pioneer and perfecter of faith.
>
> For the joy that was set before him he endured the cross, scorning its shame, and sat down at the right hand of the throne of God.
> Consider him who endured such opposition from sinners, so that you will not grow weary and lose heart.
>
> In your struggle against sin, you have not yet resisted to the point of shedding your blood.
>
> Endure hardship as discipline; God is treating you as his children. God disciplines us for our good, in order that we may share in his holiness.
>
> No discipline seems pleasant at the time, but painful. Later on, however, it produces a harvest of righteousness and peace for those who have been trained by it.
>
> Hebrews 12:1-4, 7, 10 & 11

The encouragement is three-fold. The first is to fix our eyes on Jesus. When we are in pain it can sometimes be hard to fix our thoughts and emotions on anything other than the pain. Despite this, the encouragement is to be focused on Jesus, the Good Shepherd who knows how best to lead us in a time of need.

Secondly, we are to consider Jesus and his example of how he endured suffering (Isa. 53:3). His example shows us how to not grow weary or give up hope. We can share in his joy that enabled him to endure the cross (Jas. 1:2-3). The joy of winning back souls and living with his people in safety for all eternity (Heb. 2:10).

Thirdly, we are to regard hardship as discipline because it affirms that we are his children, even though it is unpleasant at the time. Though this may seem contrary to what should be the case, we can choose to endure hardship and learn from it. We share in his sufferings so we can share in his glory (Rom. 8:17).

Jesus is *the* example of how to live through suffering. The apostle Peter says "if you suffer for doing good and you endure it, this is commendable before God. To this you were called, because Christ suffered for you, leaving you an example, that you should follow in his steps." (1 Pet. 2:20-21).

Carrying our scars

Jesus' death on the cross would have been deeply and extremely traumatic (Heb. 2:17). In his resurrected body he had scars on his hands, feet and side (Lk. 24:39). He is called the Lamb that was slain (Rev. 7:9–10, 17). He carries the scars of his trauma and sacrifice for all eternity. Even with a resurrected body, he chose to keep the scars.

It is important to recognise that post-trauma, we are likely to be different. We can heal from the trauma but it will most likely leave scars. The scars left by trauma may be with us for the rest of our lives. It is unlikely that we can completely go back to the way we were and may therefore need to create a new normal.

The scars from trauma can be physical, emotional and/or psychological. Trauma may also leave us physically or mentally changed. Throughout the recovery process, we will need to incorporate the experience of trauma into our thinking, memories and faith, because it will have affected us so deeply.

We have a choice after trauma to cultivate growth – post-traumatic growth (PTG). This allows us to get rid of any clutter left over from the traumatic experience or from how we respond to it. PTG is positive psychological change experienced as a result of difficult and traumatic events.

Growth does not occur as a direct result of trauma; rather, it is the individual's journey with the new reality in the aftermath of trauma that is crucial in determining the extent to which post-traumatic growth occurs. Research estimates that half to two-thirds of people experience PTG.[104]

PTG "involves 'life-changing' psychological shifts in thinking and relating to the world and the self, that contribute to a personal process of change, that is deeply meaningful".[105] Growth can occur in five areas – personal strength, new possibilities, improved relationships, appreciation for life and spirituality.[106]

Dr Tedeschi, Professor of Psychology at the University of North Carolina (USA) says "People develop new understandings of themselves, the world they live in, how to relate to other people, the kind of future they might have and a better understanding of how to live life."

---

[104] Collier, Lorna. "Growth after trauma". *APA*. https://www.apa.org/monitor/2016/11/growth-trauma
[105] Tedeshi, R.G., & Calhoun, L.G. *Posttraumatic Growth: Conceptual Foundation and Empirical Evidence*. Philadelphia, PA: Lawrence Erlbaum Associates, 2004.
[106] Tedeschi, Richard. "Growth After Trauma". *Harvard Business Review*. https://hbr.org/2020/07/growth-after-trauma

Trauma does not need to be the end of the story but can be the beginning of a new one. As with any growth, PTG is a natural process and can't be rushed. As we go through PTG we are likely to identify some positive reactions and learnings from the traumatic events. This can add new strength and encouragement for the life ahead.

We explored Joseph's story in the chapter *Be Quick To Forgive* and how he was betrayed, enslaved, falsely accused and oppressed. Despite this, he was able to see a different perspective and saw that even though it was meant to harm him, God intended it for good by saving many lives from famine (Gen. 50:20).

Maybe we can use our experience of trauma to save lives. PTG can in time allow us to help others in their recovery and walk alongside them in their difficult journey. We can bring hope, encouragement and friendship, showing them there can be life after trauma. Author C.S. Lewis said, "Hardship often prepares an ordinary person for an extraordinary destiny."

Staying close to God

Pain and suffering can be the hardest moments in people's lives and many will require the encouragement of family and friends to help develop the strength, resilience and patience required. There may be times when the pain feels overwhelming and too much to bear. There are likely to be times when God feels far away.

During a time of suffering, there are times when we can make choices to stop the experience of affliction from becoming internal clutter that creates distance between us and God. This is a genuinely difficult journey because it can challenge our beliefs about who God is and what we expect of him.

Yet if we want more of God in our lives, when we suffer, we need to find the compass that allows us to navigate such experiences. We need to be realistic about how difficult such as journey can be. Jesus, our Shepherd, knows how to sustain us on such a difficult journey, so we need to choose daily to stay as close as we can to him.

Helen Keller, a world-famous author, speaker, and advocate for people with disabilities, who lost her sight and hearing at nineteen months old, said "Character cannot be developed in ease and quiet. Only through experience of trial and suffering can the soul be strengthened, ambition inspired, and success achieved."

Will we make space for Jesus by asking him to help us work through any clutter related to suffering?

Reflection

Consider these verses:

> *In bringing many sons and daughters to glory, it was fitting that God, for whom and through whom everything exists, should make the pioneer of their salvation perfect through what he suffered.*
>
> Hebrews 2:10

Ask Father God:

- Lord, how can I fix my eyes on Jesus?
- Lord, have I given up my hope or got lost whilst walking through painful times in my life?
- Lord, have I condemned myself when I have found it difficult to cope with suffering?

Prayer:

Thank you Jesus because you suffered, I can be forgiven and set free from sin. Thank you for your example of how to endure in suffering.

As the good shepherd, show me how to understand that you are my compass during my suffering.

To do:

- If you are experiencing suffering, do you need to seek professional help to process your suffering and trauma?
- If you have a loved one who is suffering, do you need to ask a group of family and friends to support you?
- If you know someone who is suffering, why not reach out to them and encourage them?

Further reading:

- Psalm 91
- 1 Peter 5:6-9
- James 1:1-5

PART TWO
FINDING JESUS

We rise by bowing, we live by dying.

When we give what we could never keep, we gain what we will never lose.

Only You can take brokenness and make it something beautiful.

We'll walk on the water with our eyes on the Father, nothing is impossible.

I'll follow You anywhere. I'll follow You anywhere you wanna go.

We Rise, Jonathan Helser

WHERE IS JESUS?

Nothing is more practical than finding God, that is, than falling in love in a quite absolute final way.
(Pedro Arrupe, Priest)

"Why are you crying?"

In 1995 we both joined a short-term mission team to Hong Kong, which was organised by the church network we were part of at the time. There were about twenty of us on the team and everyone was excited about what God was going to do in the next three weeks. We were also excited about travelling to the other side of the world.

We were visiting Hang Fook camp in Kowloon to work with St. Stephen's Society which provides rehabilitation homes for recovering drug addicts, ex-prostitutes, and ex-gang members.[107] This charity was started in 1981 by Jackie Pullinger and the stories we had read in her book *Chasing the Dragon* were both amazing and challenging. [108]

During our time there we spent a week in a house dedicated to helping people recover from the multiple consequences of heroin addiction. Over the first two days there I (Mark) felt awful – it was a combination of feeling empty, hopeless, lonely

---

[107] St. Stephens Society. https://www.ststephenssociety.com
[108] Pullinger, Jackie. *Chasing The Dragon.* Hodder & Stoughton, 1980.

and a failure. I couldn't understand why I felt this way and thought these feelings were spoiling my trip abroad.

After praying with Fiona, I understood that Father God was letting me feel what some of the recovering addicts were feeling. This is the first time this had ever happened to me, but is something that continues to happen. Even now this taught me that Father God wants to share his compassion with us all for people with brokenness, which is one of the ways we learn what is important to him.

One evening there was a gathering of some of the recovering addicts together for a Bible study and prayer. One of the senior leaders of the ministry was visiting the house and invited us both to join the meeting. He was very hospitable and helped translate some of the conversations so we could understand what was going on.

Towards the end of the meeting, several of us shared some prophetic words for healing that God had given us.[109] At this point in our Christian lives, miraculous healing was predominantly something we heard about rather than experienced. We sometimes prayed for each other when one of us had a headache and occasionally saw God heal it.

There was excitement in the meeting as people responded to these prophetic words, but we couldn't really tell what was going on because they were all speaking Cantonese. At this point, I (Mark) needed the toilet and left the room. As I returned from the toilet, one of the recovering drug addicts was walking towards me.

---

[109] Prophetic words for healing are given by God to a Christian to indicate his intent to heal someone. These words are typically heard, felt or thought.

I noticed he was crying and that his nose was running, yet he seemed happy. I asked him "Why are you crying?". He replied, "Because my nose is running!". I didn't understand why this was significant, but he explained that snorting drugs had damaged his nasal passages and as a consequence, he had not had a running nose in years!

I was speechless! God has just rebuilt and repaired this man's nasal septum and put it back to normal after a simple prayer! I stood there happy but in shock, not knowing what to say, which was probably not the response he was looking for! Jesus tells us that all things are possible, but at that moment I realised that I did not always believe that (Mt. 19:26).

A new normal

For the three weeks we were in Hong Kong we saw miracles like this *nearly every day*. This included seeing a man physically withdraw from heroin addiction with only minor sickness through being prayed for by teams of people (including us) in four-hour shifts for several days.

Ex-addicts who had gone to government clinics described heroin withdrawal involving piercing headaches, hallucinations, intense abdominal pain, nausea, vomiting, diarrhoea, itchy skin, burning sensations, restlessness, hot and cold flushes, tremors, chronic insomnia and painful muscle cramps. Miraculously, the people we prayed for didn't experience these symptoms. We also saw people become Christians almost every day we were there.

This was a truly profound experience for us both that shaped us for life. We found Jesus in Hong Kong in a way we had not found him back home. We did not understand at the time why this was and we had so many questions. This experience created a hunger in us for more of God, but we had no idea what to do about it.

When we returned home, we could not cope with our church services. It was not that the church we went to was bad, actually, it was very good. But we could not deal with the disparity between experiencing the tangible presence of God in sung worship and not regularly seeing miracles and people saved as we had done in Hong Kong. It was like a reverse culture shock.

We cried in our church service most weeks for months as we struggled to adjust to a different norm from the one that we had left. For the next few years, whenever Jackie Pullinger came to the UK, we would go and hear her speak. We could not get away from this new norm of God regularly miraculously working.

At times we suppressed it; for years we did not understand it. Sometimes it led to discouragement and discontentment. Yet God was at work within us. He was shaping us for his purpose and challenging our beliefs. The main issue at the time was that we had no peers who could help us with what we were experiencing.

About a year after we visited Hong Kong, Jackie was speaking at a church in London on a Saturday. We both went to listen and we responded to an invitation to be prayed for at the end of the meeting. I (Mark) don't remember who prayed for me or what was said, but the next morning I woke up with five very specific prophetic words in my mind.

This was new to me, it had not happened before. I had specific information about people and situations in their lives. As it was a Sunday, we got up and went to church and I tentatively shared these during the service. To my surprise, five people responded, and the prophetic words were all accurate.

What was interesting about these five prophetic words was that one was for a non-Christian, one for someone who was marginalised and the other three for deep needs and concerns within Christians. We began to understand that God misses nothing. He has compassion for everyone, but especially for those who are struggling and those on the edge of society.

We also started to learn that God wants to work in us and through us all to help anyone that God has compassion for. These are often people that society regards as overlooked and powerless. It is in the lives of people like this that God wants to do the impossible, it is in people like this that God wants to experience the transforming power of his kingdom.

Finding Jesus

Where's Wally? (or Waldo in the USA and Canada) is a series of children's puzzle books which consist of several detailed double-page spread illustrations depicting lots of people doing a variety of amusing things at a given location. Readers are challenged to find a character named Wally hidden among the people.

There is a similar book called Finding Jesus, where readers are challenged to find Jesus in a multitude of unexpected places such as crowded rock concerts, bustling supermarkets and packed weddings.[110] The book introduction says, "While finding Jesus isn't necessarily easy, it's never been more fun".

---

[110] Rowntree, Winston. *Finding Jesus*. Square Peg, 2014.

Jesus' rabbinic call, saying 'follow me' to people, was to choose them as his disciples so that they could become *like him*. Jesus underlines this in a conversation with his disciples about forgiveness. He says "The student is not above the teacher, but everyone who is fully trained will be like their teacher." (Lk. 6:40).

If we want the fullness of God in our lives then we need to become more like Jesus.[111] This means being like, thinking like and having the same priorities as Jesus. Jesus invites us all to follow him as his apprentice. It is the best way to find out what he is like, what is important to him, and how to develop a lifestyle like his.

If we asked you what is the pinnacle of the Christian experience, what would you answer? There are many different ways to answer this question. We have noticed that there is an increasing trend to ask for more of God in corporate sung worship. Whilst worshipping, Christians are often excited about experiencing the tangible presence of God.

Experiencing the love of God is an important aspect of what it means to be a Christian. Having our identity rooted and established in the love of God is crucial to being filled with the fullness of God (Eph. 3:14-21). Yet are we becoming consumers of God's presence for personal benefit alone? Is the height of the Christian experience corporate sung worship or is it something else?

On the last and greatest day of the Jewish feast Sukkot, which is also called the Feast of Tabernacles, Jesus stood and said loudly "Let anyone who is thirsty come to me and drink. Whoever

---

[111] This does not mean being like Jesus in his divinity but to live like him in his humanity, because Jesus is the perfect image of a human being as well as a perfect image of God.

believes in me, as Scripture has said, rivers of living water will flow from within them." (Jn. 7:37-38).

This feast is primarily about commemorating the Exodus from Egypt and the dependence of the people of Israel on God (Lev. 23:42-43). Significant moments of Jesus' life occurred at Jewish feasts such as his death at the Passover and the coming of the Holy Spirit at Shavuot (Pentecost). His words at Sukkot are also significant.

Firstly, Jesus' use of the phrase "living water" can be found in the messianic prophecies in Zechariah 14, which is why some of his hearers said he was the Messiah (Jn. 7:41). The practice of the feast was to gather water from the pool of Siloam and bring it to the temple, so on the last day of the feast it would be poured out on the altar as an offering to God.

Imagine the scene as the feast reaches its climax. The priests circled the altar seven times with great pomp and ceremony shouting "Hosanna", which means save and deliver.[112] As they pour the water on the altar as an appeal to God, Jesus stands and says he is the source of the real living water! By saying this, Jesus is communicating that he is their God and their Messiah.[113]

Secondly, John interprets the event for us and says, "by this he meant the Spirit, whom those who believed in him were later to receive." (Jn. 7:39). This time it is not natural water that is poured out on the Temple altar, rather it is the Holy Spirit that is poured out on the altar of our lives.

---

[112] Strongs H3467
[113] Klett, Fred. "Sukkot: A Promise of Living Water". *Jews For Jesus*. https://jewsforjesus.org/blog/sukkot-a-promise-of-living-water

Yet what is the purpose of us receiving the Holy Spirit? Is it just to enjoy experiencing God's love in corporate sung worship? Worship in the Bible refers to loud celebration, praise, dance, bowing down, adoration, thanksgiving and singing. Worship from a Hebrew perspective also means service to others and daily work.[114] Do we make time to serve people in our communities as part of our regular expression of worship?

Theologian John Piper says "The inner essence of worship is to know God truly and then respond from the heart... by valuing God, treasuring God, prizing God, enjoying God, being satisfied with God above all earthly things. And then that deep, restful, joyful satisfaction in God overflows in... demonstrable acts of love in serving others for the sake of Christ." [115]

Therefore our worship is about how we live our whole life, not just when we are at church or a Christian event. We show our worship to God in our daily work, service to others, and loving people. Worship includes making space in our lives for what is most important to God, which Jesus models to us.

The family business

Good fathers don't only show their love for their children by providing for them. They also establish their identity, help them identify their strengths and equip them to live a fulfilled life. Father God wants us to feel secure in his love, but he also wants to equip us so we can join him in his chief purpose of reconciling the world to himself (2 Cor. 5:19).

---

[114] Burkhart, Austin. "'Avodah': What It Means to Live a Seamless Life of Work, Worship, and Service". *Institute for Faith, Work & Economics*. https://tifwe.org/avodah-a-life-of-work-worship-and-service

[115] Piper, John. "What is worship?". Desiring God https://www.desiringgod.org/interviews/what-is-worship

WHERE IS JESUS?

As God's children, we get invited into the *family business* which is to seek and save the lost (Lk. 19:10). We become Jesus's brothers and sisters by doing the will of our Father in heaven (Mt. 12:48-50). As family members, we get to work in his vineyard (Mt. 20:1-16) and working is part of our worship as much as sung worship is.

True worship is to surrender ourselves to God and make him the greatest focus and priority of our lives. This requires us to bow down and serve his redemptive plan for mankind. True worship is also to become like Jesus and live a lifestyle of servitude like his, based on his priorities. The invitation to such a lifestyle is the greatest invitation any of us will ever receive.

Jesus said, "the Son can do nothing by himself; he can do only what he sees his Father doing, because whatever the Father does the Son also does." (Jn. 5:19). If we want to find Jesus, we need to look where he is when he joins in with what the Father is already doing. That way Jesus' lifestyle can become our lifestyle.

Finding Jesus is not hard when we know where to look for him. Unfortunately, we often look for him in the wrong places and get disappointed or discouraged. If we don't find him where we expect to, maybe it is because we are not looking in the right places. Jesus' priorities are not a mystery; he has made them clear to us.

To fully grasp Jesus' priorities we need to not just look at how he changes someone's life in a Bible story but also consider the person's circumstances, their place in society and how their culture would have treated them. In reading the Bible this way, it enables us to see that Jesus can be found in several key places, showing us his priorities.

Finding Jesus and joining him in these places will lead to us experiencing the more of God that we desire. The apostle Paul says, "For in Christ all the fullness of the Deity lives in bodily form, and in Christ you have been brought to fullness." (Col. 2:9-10). Jesus' example shows us how to live in the fullness of God.

Douglas J. Moo says "All that human beings can know or experience of God is found in Christ, and so Christians, simply by virtue of being Christians, have access to all this knowledge and all these experiences. We need look nowhere else... that fullness is ours because we are 'in' Christ".[116]

Craig S. Keener says, "Whatever the precise sense Paul means by "fullness," he clearly means that access to all that God is and does is available only through Christ".[117] But how do we access this fullness? Do we get it automatically when we become a Christian or does it require something of us to grow into?

This fullness includes being buried with him in baptism, being raised with him to a new life, and being forgiven of all our sins (Col. 2:11-12). So encouragingly, we can experience this fullness when we become Christians. Yet Paul also talks about the need for the body of Christ to become mature.

It is this maturity that enables us collectively to attain "to the whole measure of the fullness of Christ" (Eph. 4:13). So we all need each other and the influence of apostles, prophets, evangelists, pastors and teachers to grow into maturity.[118] These

---

[116] Moo, Douglas. The Letters to the Colossians and to Philemon (The Pillar New Testament Commentary). Eerdmans, 2008.

[117] Keener, Craig. The IVP Bible Background Commentary: New Testament. Inter-Varsity Press, 2014.

[118] Church denominations may have different perspectives on the role and function of the Ephesian 4 gifts. The emphasis here is their place in equipping Christians and churches so they can reach unity, become mature and attain to the whole measure of the fullness of Christ.

gifts of people to the church help us understand who Jesus is, how to become like him, his priorities and where to find him.

The majority of Jesus' interactions with people in the Gospels, along with the apostle's letters, clearly show us Jesus' priorities and where he can be found. There are five primary places where we will find Jesus: in the Bible, in the church, in ourselves, among the lost and among the marginalised.

Jesus explained to two of his disciples on the Emmaus road "what was said in all the scriptures concerning himself" (Lk. 24:27). The Apostle Paul tells us that the church is a place where believers are "built together to become a dwelling in which God lives by his Spirit." (Eph. 2:22). Paul also tells us that "the glorious riches of this mystery, which is Christ in you, the hope of glory" (Col. 1:27).

Matthew's gospel finishes with a promise from Jesus that as we join him in the Great Commission he is with us "always, to the very end of the age" (Mt. 28:20). When Jesus tells the parable of the Sheep and the Goats, he said that when they share with someone in need "you did it for me" (Mt. 25:40). Here, Jesus is identifying with the poor, naked and imprisoned.

These are the places that we are invited by Jesus to regularly find him in. As we find him in these places, we can start to develop a Jesus-like lifestyle around each one of these places. This will take us on a journey to become more like Jesus. As we emulate Jesus, we get to be transformed into his image (2 Cor. 3:18). In this part of the book we will explore each one of these places in further detail.

A life of impact

As human beings, our growth and development are influenced by our parents and genetic composition. When we are born again, our spiritual genetics change so that we have God's nature within us (2 Pet. 1:4). That enables God to work within our inmost being to change us from the inside out.

It is important to note that it is not just about what we believe, it is also about what we do – our beliefs are meant to lead to action. The Apostle James wrote "Show me your faith without deeds, and I will show you my faith by my deeds." (Jas. 2:18). This is the test of our discipleship because Jesus said the kingdom of God is to be demonstrated not just talked about (1 Cor. 4:20).

The Holy Spirit is not just meant to affect us personally, but also to flow out of our lives like rivers of living water to our Christian brothers and sisters, the unsaved, the poor and the marginalised. Jesus says to all his disciples "Freely you have received; freely give." (Mt. 10:8).

The river that Ezekiel saw in a vision coming out from the temple was moving East (Ez. 47:1-12). This is the same direction that Adam went when he was driven out of the Garden of Eden (Gen. 3: 24). This direction is then perhaps symbolic of mankind moving away from God.

In the vision, the further the river travelled East, the deeper it got (Ez. 47:3-6). The river's depth likely symbolises a place where the more of God can be found. If we want to experience the fullness of God, we will need to leave the safety of the church and go where the river is deepest. Ezekiel was asked "do you see this?" (Ez. 47:6) – do we need to ask ourselves whether we see the significance of this?

WHERE IS JESUS?

When the river reached the Dead Sea, it turned the salty water into fresh water (Ez. 47:8). This could mean that even the worst places and people in the world are not beyond God's help. Those who have travelled furthest from God are still within reach of his salvation! Do we need to challenge our preconceptions and subconscious ideas about who is likely, or not, to respond to the gospel?

Bishop David Sheppard wrote, "The Gospel is both about changing people from inside out and changing the course of events to set people free." [119] Our Christian lives cannot be simply defined by the effect that God has in our personal lives. Our lives also need to be defined by the impact that God has on others by his work in and through us.

One of the primary reasons we are baptised with the Holy Spirit (Acts 1:4-8) is so that we can become like Jesus and do the things that Jesus did (Lk. 4:18-19). That is the goal of discipleship, that when people meet us, they encounter Jesus. The Christian experience is to become like Jesus in thoughts, words and deeds.

When the water was being poured out at Sukkot, it was a spectacle, visible to all who were watching. This ceremony was not hidden away in the corner, it was an annual event to be witnessed by the whole community. The same is meant to be true when we are filled with the Holy Spirit; the world around us is meant to be positively impacted by Christ on display in us.

Jesus's strategy to change the world is focused on us, his disciples. Despite our weakness at times, Jesus chose us to complete the Great Commission. We are his first choice because of his ability to work in and through us. God has not made a

---

[119] Sheppard, David. Bias to the Poor. Hodder & Stoughton, 1984.

mistake, he knows what he is doing and his strategy is a well-considered plan.

His plan is genius because he can work through millions of Christians every day so that vast numbers of unsaved and marginalised people can experience his love and miraculous power. His plan is for the world to encounter millions of disciples that represent him in thought, word and deed. That is why he invites us to follow him and go to the places where he goes.

A few days before his death, Jesus said these challenging words: "Anyone who loves their life will lose it, while anyone who hates their life in this world will keep it for eternal life. Whoever serves me must follow me; and where I am, my servant also will be. My Father will honour the one who serves me." (Jn. 12:25-26).

If we want to experience the fullness of God, we need to serve Jesus and his priorities and go where Jesus is. To find more of God we need to find where Jesus is and join him there. Joining in with what God is already doing in the lives of people is the best way to experience more of him.

Do we want more of God? If so, will we invite him to be at work in us, so we become more like Jesus?

Reflection

Consider these verses:

> *The word of the Lord came to Jonah son of Amittai: "Go to the great city of Nineveh and preach against it, because its wickedness has come up before me." But Jonah ran away from the Lord and headed for Tarshish. He went down to Joppa, where he found a ship bound for that port.*
>
> Jonah 1:1-3

Ask Father God:

- Lord, are there any places you want me to go that I am running away from?
- Lord, where have I already joined you in a place where you are?
- Lord, is there a specific place that you are inviting me to join you in?

Prayer:

> *Thank you for your invitation to go where you are. Please show me the people and places where I can go to, to find you. Help me understand what your priorities are and how I can position myself to enjoy your fullness.*

To do:

- Recall testimonies of where the Holy Spirit has flowed through you to the lives of others.
- If you have not been baptised in the Holy Spirit, why not ask him to do this now?
- Explore further what it means to be a disciple of Jesus in thought, word and deed.

Further reading:

- John 12:23-26
- Matthew 12:46-50
- Jonah 3:1-10

JESUS IN THE BIBLE

The Bible is the greatest of all books;
to study it is the noblest of all pursuits;
to understand it, the highest of all goals.
(Charles Ryrie, Theologian)

It's all about Jesus

This may feel like a strange question, but have you ever wondered *why* we read the Bible? Is it there just to provide moral guidance or is its purpose to challenge us to live in a way that runs counter to the culture we live in?[120] Even though these are good reasons to read the Bible, do we read the Bible just to become better people?

A Bible Society survey in 2021 found that reading the Bible during the Coronavirus pandemic had a positive effect on people's mental wellbeing.[121] The same survey also reported that reading the Bible had increased people's confidence in their future. These benefits are important but do we read the Bible just to strengthen ourselves?

---

[120] 73% agreed with this in a 2008 Evangelical Alliance survey. "Attitudes to the Bible". *Evangelical Alliance.* https://www.eauk.org/church/research-and-statistics/attitudes-to-the-bible.cfm
[121] Southam, Hazel. "Christians are gaining hope and confidence during the pandemic through reading the Bible, a survey finds". *Bible Society.*
https://www.biblesociety.org.uk/latest/news/christians-are-gaining-hope-and-confidence-during-the-pandemic-through-reading-the-bible-a-survey-finds

Reading the Bible can help us in so many ways. It can encourage us, bring us peace, help us grow spiritually, strengthen our faith, provide guidance, give us wisdom, convict us of sin and so much more. There are many reasons to read the Bible, but are we missing something?

After Jesus' resurrection, Jesus joined two of his disciples on a road a few miles from Jerusalem, who were on their way to Emmaus. The two disciples were talking with each other about everything that had recently happened, including Jesus' death and the empty tomb. They were most likely travelling home after Passover.

They were downcast and were discouraged and confused by the recent events. Jesus unexpectedly meets them on the road, but they do not recognise him. They ask Jesus if he knew about the things that had been happening in Jerusalem. Jesus responds with another question:

> 'What things?' he asked.
>
> 'About Jesus of Nazareth,' they replied. 'He was a prophet, powerful in word and deed before God and all the people. The chief priests and our rulers handed him over to be sentenced to death, and they crucified him; but we had hoped that he was the one who was going to redeem Israel. And what is more, it is the third day since all this took place.
>
> In addition, some of our women amazed us. They went to the tomb early this morning but didn't find his body. They came and told us that they had seen a vision of angels, who said he was alive. Then some of our companions went to the tomb and found it just as the women had said, but they did not see Jesus.'

He said to them, 'How foolish you are, and how slow to believe all that the prophets have spoken! Did not the Messiah have to suffer these things and then enter his glory?' And beginning with Moses and all the Prophets, he explained to them what was said in all the Scriptures concerning himself.

As they approached the village to which they were going, Jesus continued on as if he were going further. But they urged him strongly, 'Stay with us, for it is nearly evening; the day is almost over.' So he went in to stay with them.

When he was at the table with them, he took bread, gave thanks, broke it and began to give it to them. Then their eyes were opened and they recognised him, and he disappeared from their sight. They asked each other, 'Were not our hearts burning within us while he talked with us on the road and opened the Scriptures to us?'

They got up and returned at once to Jerusalem. There they found the Eleven and those with them, assembled together and saying, 'It is true! The Lord has risen and has appeared to Simon.' Then the two told what had happened on the way, and how Jesus was recognised by them when he broke the bread.

Luke 24:19-35

The two disciples, one who was named Cleopas, would have known the Torah in depth, including the messianic prophecies, having learned it from an early age.[122] Despite this, they could not connect their understanding of the Torah with recent events.

---

[122] The books of Genesis, Exodus, Leviticus, Numbers and Deuteronomy

Jesus arrives and points out that they are slow to believe what the prophets have spoken.

What happens next must have been amazing for them. He joins all the dots for them. Jesus gives them a personal walkthrough of the Scriptures to help them see that is he who they hoped he was. Imagine this moment – Jesus himself made time to explain so much to two of his discouraged disciples. He also points out they had not understood that the Messiah needed to suffer.

What Jesus did here, helps us understand one of the main reasons why we read the Bible: "And beginning with Moses and all the Prophets, he explained to them what was said in all the Scriptures concerning himself." (Lk. 24:27). Jesus wants us to read the Bible to understand who he is, what he has achieved and what the implications are for us.

Jesus is saying it is all about him. There is no one more important, more interesting or more significant in the universe than Jesus. Studying this unique God-man is the only way to understand the universe, its reason for existence and the purpose of humanity. The trouble is, like Cleopas and his friend, we can be slow to believe what the Bible says.[123]

Once the two disciples realise that it was Jesus that was with them, he disappears! Yet their response is not negative, rather they discuss how their hearts were burning within them.[124] This is what happens when we truly understand who Jesus is and what the implications are for ourselves and the whole world.

The above situation is not the only incident where Jesus says the Scriptures are about him. The Jewish leaders often opposed

---

[123] Boa, Kenneth. "The God-Man". *Bible.org*. https://bible.org/article/god-man
[124] Strong's G2545

Jesus because he healed people on the Sabbath. In response, Jesus said he was equal to God and said that God, his father, was working on the Sabbath and had sent him to miraculously heal people (Jn. 5:17-19).

Jesus then says to the Jewish leaders that the scriptures testify about him:

> 'If I testify about myself, my testimony is not true. There is another who testifies in my favour, and I know that his testimony about me is true.
>
> 'You have sent to John and he has testified to the truth. Not that I accept human testimony; but I mention it that you may be saved. John was a lamp that burned and gave light, and you chose for a time to enjoy his light.
>
> 'I have testimony weightier than that of John. For the works that the Father has given me to finish – the very works that I am doing – testify that the Father has sent me. And the Father who sent me has himself testified concerning me. You have never heard his voice nor seen his form, nor does his word dwell in you, for you do not believe the one he sent. You study the Scriptures diligently because you think that in them you have eternal life. These are the very Scriptures that testify about me, yet you refuse to come to me to have life.
>
> 'I do not accept glory from human beings, but I know you. I know that you do not have the love of God in your hearts. I have come in my Father's name, and you do not accept me; but if someone else comes in his own name, you will accept him. How can you believe since you accept glory from one another but do not seek the glory that comes from the only God?

'But do not think I will accuse you before the Father. Your accuser is Moses, on whom your hopes are set. If you believed Moses, you would believe me, for he wrote about me. But since you do not believe what he wrote, how are you going to believe what I say?'

John 5:31-47

In verse 39 Jesus says that the scriptures testify about *him* and in verse 46 he says that Moses wrote about *him*. When we read the Bible we can at times miss *who* it is about. Whilst reading the Bible we can develop theology, enjoy adventurous stories, and be inspired by stand-out characters. Yet we can miss its chief purpose – it all points to Jesus.

Finding Jesus in the Bible

The apostle John tells us that Jesus was there in the beginning, through him, all things were made and that he is the light of the world (Jn. 1:1-3 & 8:12). Jesus is also the judge of the world and the King of Kings (Rev. 20:12 & 19:16). Jesus is the image of the invisible God and he makes it possible for God to live among people (Col. 1:15 & Rev. 21:3).

Our lives only make sense if we understand who Jesus is, what he has done and what that means for us and the world. If we want more of God in our lives, we can only do that by learning to be a disciple of Jesus. To be a disciple of Jesus is to learn to be like him, which is why we need to understand that the Bible is about *him*.

Dr Christopher Chavasse puts it like this: "The Bible is the portrait of our Lord Jesus Christ. The gospels are the figure itself in the portrait. The Old Testament is the background leading up to the divine figure, pointing towards it and absolutely necessary to the composition as a whole. The church letters (epistles) serve as the dress and accoutrements of the figure, explaining and describing it. Then, while by our Bible reading we study the portrait as a great whole, the miracle happens, the figure comes to life and stepping down from the canvas of the written word, the everlasting Christ... becomes himself our Bible teacher, to interpret to us in all the Scriptures the things concerning himself."

It is important to realise that when Jesus said the scriptures testified about him he was referring to the Old Testament, as the New Testament didn't yet exist. That is all the Old Testament books, which include law, history, wisdom and prophets. All these books help us understand Jesus, what is important to him and what his priorities are.

We may struggle with some bits of the Old Testament. Maybe because of the seeming inequality between men and women, the minute detail in the laws, the use of animal sacrifices, or the amount of violence and killing All these things when taken in context can help us in our understanding of who Jesus is, what he achieved through his death, and what kind of life we should live.

The Apostle Paul wrote "For everything that was written in the past was written to teach us, so that through the endurance taught in the Scriptures and the encouragement they provide we might have hope." (Rom 15:4). We neglect reading the Old Testament to our detriment.

The New Testament can also only be fully understood alongside the Old Testament. Jesus used first-century rabbinic teaching methods to bring alive the passages of scriptures to his hearers. He regularly referenced Old Testament passages to explain who he was and what was important to his Father God.

To fully understand who Jesus is and how to follow him, we need to find him in *both* the Old and New Testaments. Otherwise, we will probably develop an incomplete view of Jesus and an inaccurate view of what the Christian life is about. It requires us at times to work at understanding the Bible. A casual reading of the Bible is unlikely to bring you into all truth (Jn. 16:13).

After the death of Moses, God said to Joshua:

> Be careful to obey all the law my servant Moses gave you; do not turn from it to the right or to the left, that you may be successful wherever you go. Keep this Book of the Law always on your lips; meditate on it day and night, so that you may be careful to do everything written in it. Then you will be prosperous and successful.
>
> Joshua 1:7-8

Psalm 1 says:

> Blessed is the one who does not walk in step with the wicked or stand in the way that sinners take or sit in the company of mockers, but whose delight is in the law of the Lord, and who meditates on his law day and night.
>
> That person is like a tree planted by streams of water, which yields its fruit in season and whose leaf does not wither – whatever they do prospers.
>
> Psalm 1:1-3

Consider the verb in these two passages, they both say meditate day and night. We are not simply meant to read one chapter of the Bible each day but rather we are encouraged to give it a sustained focus so that we become familiar with what it says. The purpose of these verses is that we learn how God wants us to live and therefore thrive in all areas of life.

The purpose of meditating on the Bible is not just so that we believe the right theological truths, but that it transforms us. Ultimately the goal of meditating is to think, live, and be like Jesus. Over time the Bible can change our thinking, character, desires, priorities and actions. This will then lead to seeing more of God in our lives.

The dictionary definitions for meditation commonly include focusing thoughts, reflecting, and pondering. The Cambridge Dictionary defines it as "to think seriously about something for a long time."[125] It is also worth noting that meditation practices often include reading aloud the text.

In Hebrew the word for "meditates" in Psalm 1 doesn't just mean to meditate in our minds but also in our speech.[126] The definitions include speak, utter, declare, talk, sing and mutter. When we use multiple senses in our meditations it increases our ability to grasp what something means. Using multiple senses can also help us keep focused on the task of meditating.

Meditation in Western culture tends to focus on the self for the benefit of mindfulness, self-improvement and self-discovery. Whilst this can help remove unwanted clutter in our minds and emotions, scriptural meditation is "a path to encounter God by giving attention to His message. It involves conversation with God, including talking to Him and quietly listening to Him".[127]

---

[125] Cambridge Dictionary. https://dictionary.cambridge.org/dictionary/english/meditate
[126] hāḡâ, Strongs H1897; śîaḥ, Strong's H7878
[127] Meyer, Stan. "Finding Mindfulness in the Jewish Scriptures". *Jews For Jesus*. https://jewsforjesus.org/learn/finding-mindfulness-in-the-jewish-scriptures

When we meditate on the Bible we are not just reading people's opinions, rather we are reading the inspired word of God. The Bible should powerfully affect us: "For the word of God is alive and active. Sharper than any double-edged sword, it penetrates even to dividing soul and spirit, joints and marrow; it judges the thoughts and attitudes of the heart." (Heb. 4:12).

The apostle Paul in his letter to Timothy says, "All Scripture is God-breathed and is useful for teaching, rebuking, correcting and training in righteousness, so that the servant of God may be thoroughly equipped for every good work." (2 Tim. 3:16-17). As we meditate on the scriptures they have the power to change us to become more like Jesus.

The frequency with which we read the Bible has a measurable effect on us. A study in 2009 found that those that who engaged with the Bible at least four times a week found feeling lonely dropped 30%, anger issues dropped 32%, bitterness in relationships dropped 40%, feeling spiritually stagnant dropped 60%, viewing pornography dropped 61%, sharing your faith jumped 200% and discipling others jumped 230%.[128]

The study also found there was *not* a steady improvement per day. The level "was basically stagnant over days one and two, with a small bump on day three. But when day four was reached, the effects spiked in an astounding way."[129] Yet only 32% of Christians surveyed engaged with the Bible four or more times a week.

If we find that our lifestyle is not changing to become like Jesus', it may be because we are not spending enough time meditating

---

[128] Cole, Arnold, "Understanding the Bible Engagement Challenge: Scientific Evidence for the Power of 4". *CBE*. https://bttbfiles.com/web/docs/cbe/Scientific_Evidence_for_the_Power_of_4.pdf
[129] Martin, Jeff. "9 Tangible Benefits of Bible Reading for Your Church". *Lifeway Research*. https://research.lifeway.com/2021/01/20/9-tangible-benefits-of-bible-reading-for-your-church

on Biblical truths and submitting our thoughts, words and actions to them. If our life is not changing after an encounter with God in sung worship, it may be because we are not putting into practice what the Bible says.

Sometimes we want the easy road and do not always embrace the effort needed to change our lives to live as Jesus did. At times we can become consumers, rather than learn from Jesus how to love God and love people. We need to be honest with ourselves when we are not adjusting to Jesus' priorities after reading the Bible.

Over thirty years ago, we got married and lived together for the first time. It became quickly apparent that we were two individuals that had different perspectives on life and priorities! As every couple does, we had to either choose to live independently or take time to discover each other's hearts, motivations, passions and priorities.

Once we discovered them, we then had to choose whether we would make time for each other's priorities in our lives. If we wanted our marriage to prosper it was obvious that we needed to do this. It was not just about making space for them, but also willingly encouraging and joining in with each other's priorities.

To love Jesus means to commit ourselves to discovering his priorities and making space for them in our lives. We will take time to listen, meditate and understand what is important to him in both thought, word and deed. The Old and New Testaments have been given to us to help with this.

How is your Bible reading going? Do you study and meditate on it or do you snack, like convenience food which only gives a little nutrition? Have you got stuck in some way in your faith journey? If so, have you looked for the solution within the pages of the Bible? Do you have unanswered questions? If so, have you looked to see what Jesus says about them?

Jesus promises that if we hear his words and *put them into practice*, then our lives will be built on a rock that will stand strong in the storms of life (Mt. 7:24-29). Do we study the Bible to understand the word made flesh (Jn. 1:14), learn from him and practice what he says? Do we immerse ourselves in the Bible to become more like Jesus individually and corporately?

Despite the need to regularly engage with the Bible, it can be hard at times to read and understand in context. If we are all honest, there are times when we may struggle to find relevance to our lives and the people around us. The following Bible study lenses will help you in this regard and also to understand the original intention of the verses to those who it was written to.

1. The Cultural Lens

The Bible was written by those from an Ancient Near Eastern (ANE) culture for an audience of the same culture. If we don't seek to understand the nature of ANE culture in which Bible events happened, we will miss or misunderstand some of what is being communicated. Therefore a basic grasp of ANE culture is helpful to understand the Bible as it was intended.

Western culture has, and still does, differ from ANE culture. This can be seen in social norms, ethical values, belief systems, food, political systems and traditions. As well as the food we eat or the clothes we wear, it is also about how we think, speak and write. Often what is unsaid in a culture can be as important as what is said.

Culture is powerful as it helps us to understand and make sense of the world around us. Author Kenneth Bailey says "What lies between the lines, what is felt and not spoken, is of deepest significance. Indeed, it almost cannot be expressed because it is not consciously apprehended. What 'everybody knows' is never explained".

It also defines what the norm is in terms of thinking, feeling and behaviour. The way Jesus thinks and acts will often be counter-cultural, therefore when we become Christians, we need to renew our minds (Rom. 12:2). Without this, we will be a disciple of our culture, rather than Jesus.

In summary, Western culture values individual freedom, autonomy, and personal achievement. In contrast, ANE culture values collective harmony, family relationships and societal responsibilities. ANE culture typically prioritises the needs of the family and community over the needs of an individual.

In 2010 an influential article coined the term W.E.I.R.D. - Western, Educated, Industrialized, Rich, and Democratic, to challenge the fact that behavioural scientists published articles with the majority of samples drawn from Western societies.[130] What was their point? It was this - not everyone in the world thinks and behaves the same way.

The main differences in culture are seen in social behaviour, lifestyle, beliefs and values, and communication styles. The key point here is that the Old Testament was written in Hebrew for people who were not W.E.I.R.D. The way they thought, felt and behaved influenced the text.

The New Testament was written in Greek by Hebrew thinkers. The language of the text changed, but the cultural thinking of

---

[130] Henrich, Joseph. "The weirdest people in the world?". *NCBI.*
https://pubmed.ncbi.nlm.nih.gov/20550733

the authors didn't. Its audience was both Eastern and Western people. This can be seen when looking at the four gospels. Matthew wrote for a Jewish audience, Mark to the Roman Empire, Luke to the Greeks and John to both Greeks and Romans.[131]

When we understand who the writer is, their cultural background, and who they were writing to, it means we can apply the lens of culture to help us understand the text. Without purposely doing this, we may subconsciously apply our own cultural norms to interpret the text and miss its intended meaning. It is important to understand what the author of a text meant from their cultural perspective.

An example of this is when we read the word 'you' in the Bible. Those from Western cultures will typically read that meaning as an individual, whereas those from Eastern cultures are most likely to read it as plural.[132] The New Testament uses both singular and plural for 'you', but over two-thirds of these are plural.

This directly influences how we understand the text. So when the Bible talks about the salt of the earth (Mt. 5:13), the light of the world (Mt. 5:14), the temple of the Holy Spirit (1 Cor. 3:16) and the body of Christ (1 Cor. 12:27) 'you' in all these verses is plural. Therefore Jesus is describing a corporate rather than individual truth.

During the Sermon on the Mount, as Jesus teaches people he uses employs both singular and plural uses of 'you':

---

[131] Akin, Daniel. "Why Four Gospels?" *Daniel Akin.* https://www.danielakin.com/wp-content/uploads/old/Resource_316/Why%20Four%20Gospels.pdf

[132] Whilst this is generally true some Western languages do differentiate the singular and plural for the word 'you' – French is an example of this.

> Ask and it will be given to you; seek and you will find; knock and the door will be opened to you. For everyone who asks receives; the one who seeks finds; and to the one who knocks, the door will be opened.
>
> Matthew 7:7-8

In verse seven, which is about asking and seeking, 'you' is plural. In verse eight, which is also about asking, 'you' is singular. Therefore Jesus is saying there is an individual *and* a collective application of asking, seeking, and knocking. This is an example of how it helps to understand when the text is highlighting individual or plural responsibility.

This matters when we are trying to understand what Jesus or others are saying. Using a resource such as an Interlinear Bible allows us to see the original Hebrew and Greek and therefore quickly understand the correct use of 'you' in the text.[133]

2. The Rabbinic Lens

The rabbis of Jesus' day used a technique that was called remez.[134] In their teaching, they would refer to part of a scripture passage in a discussion, knowing that their audience's knowledge of the Bible would allow them to deduce for themselves the fuller meaning of the teaching.

Jesus regularly used this teaching method. For example, a rabbi could choose a distinctive word or phrase from a passage in the Old Testament as a way of alluding to all of the passage. So for example, when Jesus quotes Isaiah in the synagogue, he quotes

---

[133] For example, Blue Letter Bible. www.blueletterbible.org
[134] That The World May Know. "Remez". *That The World May Know.* https://www.thattheworldmayknow.com/remez

two verses from Isaiah 61 and one verse from Isaiah 58 (Lk. 4:16-19).

His hearers would have understood that he is referring to most, if not all, of Isaiah 61 and Isaiah 58. So if we read just the fifty words he speaks, we miss the full extent of what he is trying to communicate. By using this teaching method that points to the full meaning of the words used, Jesus was referring to all the words in these two chapters of Isaiah.

By doing this, Jesus is communicating what it looked like for him to be anointed with the Holy Spirit and what the kingdom of God looks like. His kingdom will focus on the poor, marginalised, broken-hearted and oppressed. A cross-reference can help us understand where a verse is pointing to and the full meaning of what is inferred.

Another example is the use of numbers in Ancient Near Eastern culture. In the account of the Tower of Babel, people tried to build a tower up to the heavens (Gen. 11:1-8). God confused their language and they could not understand each other. Based on the list of descendants of Noah in Genesis 10 it can be deduced there were 72 languages.

In Luke 10:1-24, Jesus sends out the 72 disciples to go ahead of him to every town he was planning to visit. What is the significance here of the number 72, as it is the same number used in Genesis 10? From a Hebrew perspective, this hints at righting the wrong at the Tower of Babel. Jesus is making a prophetic statement that the gospel will reconcile the nations to one another.[135]

---

[135] This can also be seen at Pentecost when people hear God in their own tongue (Acts 2:8).

Another example of the use of numbers can be found in Mark 5:21-43 which details the story of Jesus healing a girl and a woman. The story begins with a synagogue leader pleading with Jesus to come to his house to heal his daughter who is 12 years old. As they headed off a large crowd followed them and a woman who had been bleeding touched the hem of Jesus' garment.

This resulted in the woman being healed. She had suffered from bleeding for 12 years. From an Ancient Near Eastern perspective, the author may be using these two healing stories to draw out further truths. Such texts invite us to ask questions and dig a bit deeper for any further meaning.

In this story, the term 'daughter' is used twice to describe both the girl and the woman. Jesus uses the term to make the point publicly that this ceremonially unclean woman was a daughter of God and therefore has value.[136] There is a beautiful parallel here between an earthly father who wants to see his daughter healed as well as a heavenly father who also does.

The purpose here is to ask questions and ponder the text and other related texts to understand the key messages being communicated. If we just read the words and use our Western logic, we can miss parts of all of what is intended for us to understand.

The Cross-referencing helps to find the use of common numbers, names and related verses. A cross-reference also enables us to see how the Old and New Testaments are stitched

---

[136] The Greek word thygatēr can mean a daughter of God as well as a female descendant, Strong's G2364

together. This is particularly helpful when we consider rabbinic teaching methods.[137]

3. The Jesus Lens

In ANE culture the god related questions are primarily about what your god is like, or to put it another way, is your god bigger than my god? In Western culture, the god related question is primarily about whether he exists or not. The Bible's Eastern origin assumes the existence of god and does not attempt to make the case whether or not he exists.

The focus of both Old and New Testament writers is to introduce us to the God that does exist and tell us what he is like by pointing to Jesus. They do this in various ways, often by comparing Jehovah to the gods of other nations. In ANE culture, the people group that had the biggest God was to be feared the most.

One feature that set the Hebrews apart was that they did not craft images of their God because he forbade it (Ex. 20:4-6). Yet God made man and woman in his image and they are therefore his image bearers to the world (Gen. 1:27). This then hints to the future when Jesus will be born, who is the perfect image of God (Col. 1:15).

As we read the Bible, it can be helpful to ask what the text tells us about God and how he is different to other gods. This helps us build a view as to what our God is like and how we can relate to him. We need to include both Old and New Testament scriptures to gain a full understanding of God.

---

[137] Tverberg, Lois. "Jesus' Rabbinic Teaching Style". *En-Gedi.*
https://engediresourcecenter.com/2019/09/09/jesus-rabbinic-teaching-style

The Jewish people of Jesus' time seemed to focus more on sacrifice to God than on showing mercy to others. When Jesus says to them "But go and learn what this means: 'I desire mercy, not sacrifice.' For I have not come to call the righteous, but sinners." (Mt. 9:13), he is quoting the Old Testament prophet (Hos. 6:6).

The Jewish people of Jesus' day had not seemingly grasped the importance of mercy, which would be powerfully demonstrated by Jesus' forgiveness of sins and inclusion of the marginalised. Not including verses from both the Old and New Testaments to understand what God is like may lead to us having incompleteness or bias in our thinking.

Our faith is very much shaped by knowing who God is, his character and his ability. Therefore when we read the Bible we need to keep the focus on what it is telling us about Jesus and what it means for us. We want to find Jesus in the Bible to help us learn to think like him, speak like him and do what he did.

The whole Bible helps with this. It is unlikely that we will find a situation in our life where the revelation of who God is in the Bible is not able to help us. Reading the stories in the Bible or the works of Jesus or the apostle's letters to the churches will all be a source of rich information and revelation as to who God is and what life looks like for those who follow him.

If we avoid difficult books because we are not willing to put the time in to understand the context and culture it was written, we may miss some of the most amazing truths and life lessons. Do we just read our favourite books in the Bible or do we also include in our study books that require more work to understand?

People should be able to tell that we are Christians because we know the God of the Bible and therefore live differently. For example, we will not get drunk or gossip, but it will also mean that we are kind and generous to the poor.[138] If we put effort into studying all of the scriptures, we can use the Jesus lens to find him in the whole Bible and learn to be like him.

Jesus invites us on an adventurous journey to mine the riches in scripture to change our lives from the inside out.

Is his face shining?

Several countries in the world ban, control or sensor the Bible, which can lead to them being confiscated or burned.[139] Church leaders can often only obtain Bibles that are smuggled into their country. In some countries, most Christians rarely get to have their own copy, with the majority given to church leaders.

Sometimes, parts of the Bible are distributed among Christians to hand copy and share with others. It is not uncommon for a Christian in such nations to have only one page of the Bible and this is usually memorised so it cannot be taken away. Because of the scarce availability of the Bible, the value they ascribe to it is immense.

In the free world, we might have multiple printed Bibles in our homes, access to multiple Bible translations online and uncountable Bible teaching resources. Yet do we value and memorise the Bible like the persecuted Christians do? Would we risk imprisonment and death so others could read the Bible?

---

[138] Eph. 5:18, Rom. 1:29, Eph. 4:32 and Prv. 19:17

[139] Urban, David. "The Continuing Story of the Banning and Censoring of the Bible". *Online Library of Liberty.* https://oll.libertyfund.org/publications/reading-room/2023-10-05-urban-banning-and-censoring-bible

In our twenties, we had the immense privilege of meeting some Christians who were involved in Bible smuggling. They had come to pick up Bibles that had been stored in a secret location and distribute them to underground churches. If they were caught they would be severely beaten and potentially killed.

During our short time together with them, we were struck by how one of their faces was shining with what we could only describe as the glory of God. It reminded us of the Bible stories of Moses and Stephen where their faces were radiant (Ex. 34:29-35 and Acts 6:8-15). We asked each other, "Is his face shining?" We couldn't take our eyes off him.

The Hebrew word for "face" can also mean presence, so when we seek God, it is akin to seeking his face.[140] When we look deep into someone's face it can reveal much about their character and personality. When we read the Bible we want to find Jesus in it, we want to be able to see his face in the verses.

Our brief time with these radiant Christians had a profound effect on us and has regularly been a provocation to read and study the Bible. To see how people valued it when it was so scarce left us with an increased value for the Bible. At times we read the Bible and it encourages us, but there are also times when we encounter the face of Jesus.

Jesus longs for us to discover him in the pages of the Bible.

---

[140] pānîm, Strong's H6440

Reflection

Consider these verses:

> *For the word of God is alive and active. Sharper than any double-edged sword, it penetrates even to dividing soul and spirit, joints and marrow; it judges the thoughts and attitudes of the heart. Nothing in all creation is hidden from God's sight. Everything is uncovered and laid bare before the eyes of him to whom we must give account.*
>
> Hebrews 4:12-13

Ask Father God:

- Lord, what I have already understood about Jesus from reading the Bible?
- Lord, what parts of the Bible do you want me to focus on at this point in my life?
- Lord, is there anyone that I could study the Bible with?

Prayer:

> *Thank you Father for your giving us the Bible. Help me to understand the passions and motivation of your son Jesus so that I may become more like him. I pray that you give me a fuller understanding of your salvation plan that centres around King Jesus.*

To do:

- Take time to meditate on scripture, including reading the passages aloud.
- Set aside time to understand Ancient Near Eastern culture and rabbinic teaching methods.[141]
- Consider using Bible commentaries, guides and devotionals to study in more depth.

Further reading:

- John 1:1-5
- Matthew 7:24-29
- Deuteronomy 6:6–7

---

[141] For further reading we would recommend:
- The Bible Project YouTube Book Summaries, https://www.youtube.com/@bibleproject
- Bailey, Kenneth. *Jesus Through Middle Eastern Eyes: Cultural Studies In The Gospels*. SPCK Publishing, 2008.
- Fee, Gordon, *How to Read the Bible for All Its Worth*, Zondervan, 2014

JESUS IN THE CHURCH

We do not want a church that will move with the world.
We want a church that will move the world.
(G.K. Chesterton, Writer & Apologist)

What is the Church?

Asking what the church is may seem like a strange question, but the way the term is commonly used in Western culture is different from how it is defined in the Bible. Dictionaries tend to define the church as a *building* for public Christian worship, but biblically the church is defined by its *people*.[142]

It is the community of God's people that are the church, especially when they assemble together. The apostle Paul also shares this perspective when he refers to Jesus as the head of the church and the church as the body of Christ (Col. 1:18-20). Seeing the church as Jesus' household profoundly affects its identity and impact on the world.

The church is not a physical building or organisation, but a spiritual house built together by living stones – Christians (1 Pet. 2:4-10). This house becomes a dwelling place where God lives by his Spirit (Eph. 2:21-22). Though Paul uses building analogies to describe the church, he is describing something made up of people, who are Jesus's body.

---

[142] ekklēsia, Strong's G1577

It is within this context that Paul says the church – the body of Christ, can attain "to the whole measure of the fullness of Christ" (Eph. 4:13). As each part of the church does its work and exercises the gifts Jesus has given them, the church can grow "to become in every respect the mature body of him who is the head, that is, Christ" (Eph. 4:15).

Paul is saying that the fullness of God in the church looks like the body of Jesus, i.e. it functions and acts as Jesus did (Eph. 1:22-23). It is therefore something powerful when God's people are in unity because there is a maturity that we can only reach when we come together and work together to represent Christ to each other and the world (Jn. 13:35).

To put it a different way, Jesus is so unfathomable, and all-encompassing, that only in a church community, across church communities, and multiple denominations can we attempt to accurately represent his fullness. It certainly cannot be done by one Christian or one church.

Jesus' concept of church is not defined by a building. Whenever we gather, whether in small or large groups, Jesus promises to be with us (Mt. 18:15-20).[143] Whether the context is for mutual encouragement, corporate worship, Bible study, fellowship, pastoral care, equipping or evangelism – we are the place where God dwells by his Spirit.

In the chapter *Jesus In The Bible*, we discussed how in the Bible 'you' can be both singular and plural. When the plural is used by Jesus or Paul, it describes a collective truth. Even though we have Christ in us, there is a collective expression of some Biblical truths that cannot be fully seen within an individual Christian.

---

[143] The context here is church discipline of sin

For example, when we speak about the church being the temple of the Holy Spirit, that is a plural truth as it describes how we as Christians are together the dwelling place of God (1 Cor. 3:16). Also when we consider the Great Commission, truths like "you are the salt of the earth" and "you are the light of the world" have a collective impact (Mt. 5:13-14).

This is important because the full measure of such truths can only be fully seen and understood if they are embraced and demonstrated collectively by multiple Christians together. It also points to the collective activity of a church that is not all inward-facing activities, but to be a church also includes sharing our faith and engaging with the issues in society.

For example, if you are sitting in a café with two other Christians enjoying each other's company and sharing stories of what God is doing, then Jesus is among you as much as he is in a larger gathering of Christians (Mt. 18:20). Also, your conversation might be overheard by unbelievers around you and influence or interest them in Christianity.

As Jesus promises to be with us, we can therefore recognise his presence and allow his influence on what happens when we are together. This could be an inward or outward focus or both. We can't divide Jesus into separate parts. He is Jesus the apostle, pastor, prophet, teacher, and evangelist.

You could be with Christian friends out for dinner at a restaurant or café. During the evening you may speak together about what God is doing in your church. You may also encourage and sharpen each another. Yet by the end of the evening, you may also have felt Jesus' compassion for the lost and witnessed to your waiter.

When we meet together the focus should not be on who we are, what gifts we have and how experienced we may be in certain tasks. The primary focus should be on Jesus and his ability to work in and through us and to people around us. We shouldn't limit his ability to show his strength in our weakness (2 Cor. 12:9–10).

We can develop mindsets that say we are not good at this or that, but when Jesus is among us, he is able to do all things through us (Phil. 4:13). You may say of yourself that you can't hear God's voice clearly or that you do not know how to share your faith, but Jesus does. When we gather together, the collective truths of who Jesus is apply to such moments.

If we grasp that Jesus is with us whenever we are gathered together as a few or many, then such moments can be profound, not just for us, but also for people around us. We don't need to pray for Jesus to come among us because he is already here. We should thank him for being with us and ask him what he wants to do in our midst.

Do we have a mindset that we are joining in with what Jesus is already doing (Jn. 5:19)? We might have our agenda and plan, which Jesus can incorporate alongside his, but wouldn't it be better to align ourselves with Jesus' priorities? We have often been out for dinner, shopping or leisure, and because Jesus is with us, he touches people around us.

For example, we have seen him miraculously heal people we meet. Others are moved when we talk to them about what God thinks of them and how much he cares for them. It doesn't matter where we are or what we are doing, Jesus can lead us to people that he wants to do good to.

God is able to orchestrate our everyday moments and gatherings with other Christians to be so much more significant and impactful than we think they may be because, like a temple, he dwells among us and within us. God has designed it this way, to put his son Jesus front and centre in our gatherings so that others will say "God is really among you!" (1 Cor. 14:25).

Let's consider common moments when we gather as Christians to understand when Jesus is among us. The emphasis here is to understand when Jesus is present so that we won't feel alone or only be aware of our own priorities. Next time you are in one of these moments, let us endeavour to find Jesus within it.

Jesus is with us during the ordinances

Typically when Christians gather for Sunday services, one or more church ordinances are celebrated.[144] This could include ordinances such as communion, baptism, marriage and anointing people who need healing. Church denominations have different emphases on the ordinances, but most emphasise the importance of such moments and ceremonies.

Shortly before his crucifixion, Jesus wanted to celebrate Passover with them. He sent two of his disciples ahead of him to prepare the meal and a guest room (Lk. 22:7-13). This was quite a moment for Jesus because this would be the last meal he ate with them before he was crucified.

They would be focused on a meal that points to his death as *the* lamb that takes away the sins of the world:

---

[144] Ordinances emphasise an act of obedience to a command of Jesus, whereas sacraments emphasise God's blessing and grace that comes through them. Christian denominations may practice specific ordinances, sacraments or both. The emphasis in this book is that Jesus may want to do more than we expect during an ordinance or sacrament.

> When the hour came, Jesus and his apostles reclined at the table. And he said to them, 'I have eagerly desired to eat this Passover with you before I suffer. For I tell you, I will not eat it again until it finds fulfilment in the kingdom of God.'
>
> After taking the cup, he gave thanks and said, 'Take this and divide it among you. For I tell you I will not drink again from the fruit of the vine until the kingdom of God comes.'
>
> And he took bread, gave thanks and broke it, and gave it to them, saying, 'This is my body given for you; do this in remembrance of me.'
>
> Luke 22:14-19

So many things happen during this meal. Jesus helps them understand that the wine and bread represent his blood and body. He reveals that one of his disciples will betray him. He demonstrates the importance of being a servant and warns Peter he will deny him.

What can we learn from this? Jesus is doing more than one thing during this meal. He is not just teaching his disciples about his death, he is modelling servant leadership, challenging potential arrogance, helping them understand the near future and preparing Peter for his forthcoming betrayal.

When we celebrate an ordinance, Jesus will always be doing more than we may think because of his love, kindness and generosity. So if we are gathered to celebrate the baptism of a new believer, why would we not also expect Jesus to heal the sick among us? If we are gathered for a wedding, why would we not expect Jesus to do a miracle (Jn. 2:1-11)?

God is able to do so much more than we can ask or imagine because of his faithfulness to all generations (Eph. 3:20 & Deut. 7:9). Recognising that Jesus is among us during the ordinances means all things are possible (Mt. 19:26). Our church gatherings should be far from ordinary because they are a place where God dwells.

We have had the privilege of baptising people who became Christians on Alpha Courses that we ran.[145] Though this ordinance is primarily about the repentance and cleansing of sin. As people came up out of the water many were changed in ways they did not expect.[146] It was an important moment to publicly say they were a Christian but often God did more!

Those we baptised have told us that things changed in their lives following baptism. These included an end to struggles with a specific sin, healing from mental and physical health, and stopping their self-loathing. Jesus does not just want to save us from our sins but transform us into his likeness (2 Cor. 3:18).

Sometimes when we celebrate an ordinance we can approach it out of habit and forget to focus on what Jesus is doing in such moments. This may be because the way it is done might become familiar and we go through the motions without the expectancy of Jesus being with us.

Jesus is with us when reading scripture

One of the implications of living in a Western society that is so individualistic is that a lot of Bible study by Christians is personal. Whilst we should read and study the Bible as

---

[145] Alpha. alpha.org.uk
[146] Churches that we attended practiced full immersion baptism

individuals, traditional Jewish approaches to studying scripture include individuals, pairs and groups.

The Jews are well known for their love of tradition, so by the time the Talmud was completed, there were well-established ideas of how they studied the text. Also, the Jews of this time were deeply scarred by the memory of the Babylonian exile because of not following scripture. So they found powerful and innovative ways to study and understand scripture.

The goal of their study is "that the words of Torah shall be clear in your mouth so that if someone asks you something, you shall need not hesitate and then tell it to him, rather you shall tell it to him immediately."[147] This would unlikely be achievable simply by studying the Torah on your own.

Therefore Jewish Torah studies adopt multiple methods to understand the richness and meaning of the Torah's text. One of these is called Pardes which considers reading the text from four perspectives: the literal meaning, the allegorical meaning, the metaphorical meaning and the hidden meaning.[148]

Another method called Chavrusa is where pairs of students of the Torah read the text aloud to each other, which helps them analyse, question, and debate the text so that they can gain a mutual understanding of the text.[149] These discussions at times can be heated and students debate loudly with each other.

---

[147] Babylonian Talmud, Kiddushin 30a
[148] Torah Life Ministry. "PaRDeS". Torah Life Ministry.
https://torahlifeministry.com/teachings/articles/23-bible-study/64-pardes.html
[149] Rosenblum, Ilene. "Chavruta: Learning Torah in Pairs". *Chabad.org*.
https://www.chabad.org/library/article_cdo/aid/1144871/jewish/Chavruta-Learning-Torah-in-Pairs.htm

When a group of friends studied the Torah together, it is called Haverim.[150] When Jesus called his disciples friends, he was most likely referring to them as haverim because, in Jesus' day, the word had a deeper relational and discipleship making focus (Jn. 15:15). It was for those disciples who chose to be closely involved in his kingdom.

When we study the Bible in groups, we are engaging in a collective moment with other believers where Jesus will be with us. As we have Christ in us, he is also present when we study the Bible alone, but there is a more powerful dynamic when we do it in a group. A collective group understanding will be richer than one individual's perspective.

We are not describing a group where one teacher is telling everyone else what the text means, but rather where a group meets to explore each of the text's facets, like a well-cut diamond. This provides a process to collaboratively discover the full meanings of the text.

None of us are given complete wisdom and understanding of the Bible. We need to rely on Jesus among a group of us to draw out the richer meanings of the text so we can apply them to our lives. This needs to be done within the guardrails of general understanding of the text's context to avoid theological error.

Such methods also work well for family reading and studies. Helping children discuss and debate different texts is a good way to learn as over time it will build confidence in their own Biblical understanding and convictions. It will also help them explain these convictions to their parents, siblings and friends.

---

[150] Haverim Devotions. What is Haverim? Haverim Devotions. https://haverimdevotions.com/haverim

After Jesus' resurrection, he appeared among his disciples and had to understandably address their doubts:

> He said to them, 'This is what I told you while I was still with you: everything must be fulfilled that is written about me in the Law of Moses, the Prophets and the Psalms.'
>
> Then he opened their minds so they could understand the Scriptures. He told them, 'This is what is written: the Messiah will suffer and rise from the dead on the third day, and repentance for the forgiveness of sins will be preached in his name to all nations, beginning at Jerusalem. You are witnesses of these things. I am going to send you what my Father has promised; but stay in the city until you have been clothed with power from on high.'
>
> Luke 24:44-49

When Jesus is with us as we study the Bible as a group, he can open up our minds so that we can understand the scriptures. If we want to grasp this great salvation that we are part of, study the Bible together with others and engage with Jesus in your midst as you do it.

Jesus is with us during unexpected moments

There are many unexpected moments in the Bible where Jesus and his disciples come across someone who needs a miracle. In these moments Jesus or his disciples see healing, demons cast out or resurrection of the dead. During these moments people seek Jesus out, but there are times when Jesus and his disciples simply come across them.

For example:

> As Jesus approached Jericho, a blind man was sitting by the roadside begging. When he heard the crowd going by, he asked what was happening. They told him, "Jesus of Nazareth is passing by."
> He called out, "Jesus, Son of David, have mercy on me!"
>
> Those who led the way rebuked him and told him to be quiet, but he shouted all the more, "Son of David, have mercy on me!"
>
> Jesus stopped and ordered the man to be brought to him. When he came near, Jesus asked him, "What do you want me to do for you?"
>
> "Lord, I want to see," he replied.
>
> Jesus said to him, "Receive your sight; your faith has healed you." Immediately he received his sight and followed Jesus, praising God. When all the people saw it, they also praised God.
>
> Luke 18:35-43

There are people all around us in our daily lives who need a miracle to demonstrate that God is real and has compassion for them. God is able to orchestrate moments where you meet people who have a need in their life that God may have already healed or changed in your life. It is like God has arranged an unexpected moment where you are the perfect person to help with.

These moments may happen in a church building or when Christians are out and about during their daily lives. We may be alone or with a group of Christian friends, whichever one it is, these are moments where God wants other Christians or unbelievers to personally experience the reality of his kingdom.

Such moments are a privilege because God is personally inviting us into them. It is his joy to involve us in bringing the reality of his kingship to people in need. He does this so that they can discover that he and his kingdom are the pearl of great price, which they may in this moment willingly give all they have to obtain (Mt. 13:44-45).

Our gospel is not simply about repentance from sin, it is about the powerful and ever-present reality of a heavenly kingdom that changes lives for now and eternity. Our role in the Great Commission is to invite people to experience Jesus and his kingdom so they can be reconciled to him (2 Cor. 5:16-21).

If we have a paradigm that the church is centred on the people of God meeting weekly in a building, we can miss the full understanding of what the church is. The New Testament church was born at Pentecost and when the Holy Spirit came on them it was seen publicly. Peter had to explain to the crowd outside the temple what God was doing (Acts 2:14-40).

We are God's house where he dwells, but this reality is not meant to be hidden away from the world. The life of God in the people of the church is meant to be seen and experienced by unbelievers around us. The reality of God's power was so known that people would bring the sick into the streets so that Peter's shadow might fall on them and be healed (Acts 5:15).

37 of Jesus' miracles are recorded in the Gospels, but only three of them occurred in the synagogue. 7 of them happened in

people's homes, but the majority happened when Jesus was visiting towns and villages. Miracles were not contained in special church meetings and events.

When Jesus met people during his travels, in these moments he had compassion for them, often asking what *they* wanted, which was central to the moment. His divinity and humanity overflowed to those around him. Jesus invites us into an evangelistic lifestyle, so his life in us can overflow to people around us, wherever we are.

If we are to follow Jesus and want more of him, we will need to follow his example and bring the reality of his kingdom to people we meet in planned or unexpected moments. Our mindsets will not be limited to thinking that God only wants to turn up in a church meeting but that *Jesus' norm* is that he wants his power to turn up wherever we are with or without other Christians – any time, any place, anywhere!

Jesus is with us when we seek and save the lost

Shortly before Jesus ascended to heaven he left his disciples the most significant task for us as Christians – to go and make disciples of all nations, what we commonly term the Great Commission:

> Then the eleven disciples went to Galilee, to the mountain where Jesus had told them to go. When they saw him, they worshipped him; but some doubted. Then Jesus came to them and said, 'All authority in heaven and on earth has been given to me.
>
> Therefore go and make disciples of all nations, baptising them in the name of the Father and of the Son and of the Holy Spirit, and teaching them to obey

everything I have commanded you. And surely I am with you always, to the very end of the age.'

Matthew 28:16-20

In the context of this commissioning, Jesus promises to be with us, accompany us and be among us always.[151] When Jesus sends us, he doesn't stay behind and watch, he gets involved with us in the nitty-gritty of it. This is a truly profound promise!

In a survey undertaken within the UK, 43 percent of the Christians knew nothing about Jesus' Great Commission and only half think it is important to share their faith.[152] In the context of this profound promise to accompany us, how is it that Christians cannot know about Jesus' purpose for coming to earth or think it is not very important?

If we desire more of Jesus in our lives then why would we not embrace his promise to accompany us as we share our faith through our daily lives? If we asked you if would you like Jesus to accompany you throughout your life, we assume you would say "yes!", but do we apply this promise to all areas of our lives, including evangelism?

When we share our faith, for it to be effective the one person we need with us when we do it is Jesus! If we want to see people experience his love, be miraculously healed and convicted of their sins, then we need to do evangelism *partnering with* Jesus. This applies to whether we share our faith with an individual or whether a group of us team up to share our faith with others.

---

[151] meta, Strong's G3326
[152] Knox, Phil. "Only half of Christians think evangelism is important. We must equip one another to share the good news". *Premier Christianity*. https://www.premierchristianity.com/opinion/only-half-of-christians-think-evangelism-is-important-we-must-equip-one-another-to-share-the-good-news/14530.article

When Jesus told us to "go", it was not a suggestion, just a good idea, or something he hoped we would do. He was inviting us into the greatest adventure of our lives. Having witnessed to many people and led many to Christ, we have both found this to be the greatest adventure of our lives.

Maybe when you have done evangelism you didn't realise that you were doing it *with* Jesus. Maybe you thought you were not any good at it or you always feel out of your depth and alone. Whilst these are humanly understandable thoughts and feelings, sharing our faith is a co-labouring activity with Jesus.

When we pray for unbelievers to experience Jesus' tangible presence, be miraculously healed or help them hear him speak to them, none of that would work unless we were doing evangelism *with* Jesus. He knows how to seek and save the lost and so he is the person we look to learn how to do these things (Lk. 19:10).

Jesus sent his disciples out to tell people the kingdom of heaven was near and to heal the sick and raise the dead (Mt. 10:8 & Lk. 10:1). They were sent to both Jews and Gentiles, covering all ethnic groups in the known world. Without Jesus at work in us, it would be impossible to heal the sick and raise the dead, to demonstrate the nearness of his kingdom.

Evangelism has been designed by Jesus to involve us alongside him. This is our greatest privilege.[153] To be invited by Jesus himself means it is something we will delight to do, trusting in his ability to work through us. Sharing our faith does not need to be something we struggle with or find difficult.

---

[153] Gilpin, Mark & Fiona. *God's Dream Our Greatest Privilege.* Evangelism Reimagined Publishing, 2020.

Maybe it is time for each believer to re-evaluate what they think evangelism is about. If we want to be more like Jesus, then we will follow his example in how to seek and save the lost. We will also embrace *his* great commission with joy and excitement, knowing he will be with us as the body of Christ together does evangelism with him.

Jesus is with us in our speaking and teaching

In his letters to Timothy, the Apostle Paul encouraged him to devote himself to the public reading of scripture and also to preaching and teaching (1 Tim 4:13). This verse emphasises instruction, encouragement, and comfort in a stirring and persuasive manner.[154]

Our faith is based on truth and on what we believe. Establishing beliefs in the lives of Christians is a key responsibility of those who teach. These are not just about establishing sound doctrine but are in fact about who we believe in. Our core beliefs must be founded on who Jesus is and who Jesus says we are.

What we believe profoundly shapes our internal world. Psychology helps us understand how beliefs are formed and how in turn they influence our reasoning, emotions, confidence and actions. They provide a model for how we understand ourselves, the world we live in and our view of who God is, his character, nature and actions.

Our beliefs are created over time. They are formed through experiences, influences and accepting what others tell us to be true. Our beliefs can be strengthened or dismantled by positive or negative experiences. Belief is a brain function which

---

[154] paraklēsis, Strongs G3874 and didaskalia, Strongs G1319

provides meaning and value, which in turn guides our behaviour.[155]

When we become Christians we are called to repent and believe the good news (Mk. 1:15) and renew our minds (Rom. 12:2). Our conversion to Christ will therefore involve a process of changing what we believe. These verses describe a renewal, renovation, complete change of mind and a change of what we place our confidence in.[156]

The aim of any speaking and teaching we undertake is to enable the listeners to change how they think, and subsequently change their behaviour, submitting to such change through the Holy Spirit. Belief is not just about mental assent, it should result in us changing ourselves to be more like Jesus, including making space for his priorities. We can know the truth but not believe it. It is our actions (or lack of action) that show us what we believe (Mt. 7:16).

Teaching and speaking that merely informs people of a new truth or perspective is not what the Bible intends. For example, a Christian can understand that evangelism is important to God, but chooses not to engage in it because their belief about doing evangelism generates fear in them. The issue here is that their established belief system associates evangelism with fear of man, fear of failure, negative experiences and/or rejection (Prv. 29:25).

Therefore teaching and speaking is only effective if it changes our belief *about God and ourselves*. As evangelists, we can implore people to engage in the Great Commission because it is important to Jesus, but if the net result doesn't provide an

---

[155] Heinrich-Heine. "Processes of believing: Where do they come from? What are they good for?", *NCBI*.
[156] Strongs G342, Strongs G3340 and Strongs G4100

accessible alternative belief that it is in fact important, the hearers won't be able to change their internal world to willingly or intentionally share their faith with others.

We need Jesus with us during our teaching and speaking. Jesus was God's word speaking to create the universe (Gen. 1:1-24, John 1:1-3) and when Jesus spoke miracles happened (e.g. Mt. 8:13). Jesus's words have the power to change people's beliefs about him and themselves:

> Each of you should use whatever gift you have received to serve others, as faithful stewards of God's grace in its various forms. If anyone speaks, they should do so as one who speaks the very words of God. If anyone serves, they should do so with the strength God provides, so that in all things God may be praised through Jesus Christ.
>
> 1 Peter 4:10-11

This does not only apply to teaching and speaking but also to the other gifts of the spirit (1 Cor. 12:1-11). Whether we are given a message of wisdom, faith, gifts of healing, miraculous power, prophecy, distinguishing between spirits, speaking and interpretation of tongues – they all should be done as one who speaks the very words of God. Such words all need to be tested to ensure they are genuine (1 Thes. 5:19-22).

We have the power of life and death in our tongue (Prv. 18:21). When we speak and teach we should include a focus on how to change people's beliefs. This will bring new life into our emotions, thoughts and actions as we endeavour to follow Jesus more.

Jesus is with us to encourage and correct

Whilst the apostle John was exiled to the island of Patmos by the Romans, he had a vision of Jesus walking amongst seven churches:

> I, John, your brother and companion in the suffering and kingdom and patient endurance that are ours in Jesus, was on the island of Patmos because of the word of God and the testimony of Jesus. On the Lord's Day I was in the Spirit, and I heard behind me a loud voice like a trumpet, which said: 'Write on a scroll what you see and send it to the seven churches: to Ephesus, Smyrna, Pergamum, Thyatira, Sardis, Philadelphia and Laodicea.'
>
> I turned round to see the voice that was speaking to me. And when I turned I saw seven golden lampstands, and among the lampstands was someone like a son of man, dressed in a robe reaching down to his feet and with a golden sash round his chest. The hair on his head was white like wool, as white as snow, and his eyes were like blazing fire. His feet were like bronze glowing in a furnace, and his voice was like the sound of rushing waters. In his right hand he held seven stars, and coming out of his mouth was a sharp, double-edged sword. His face was like the sun shining in all its brilliance.
>
> When I saw him, I fell at his feet as though dead. Then he placed his right hand on me and said: 'Do not be afraid. I am the First and the Last. I am the Living One; I was dead, and now look, I am alive for ever and ever! And I hold the keys of death and Hades.

'Write, therefore, what you have seen, what is now and what will take place later. The mystery of the seven stars that you saw in my right hand and of the seven golden lampstands is this: the seven stars are the angels of the seven churches, and the seven lampstands are the seven churches.

Revelation 1:9-20

This is a profound revelation of the risen Christ, his golden sash most likely representing him as a priest and mediator (Lev. 8:7 & Heb. 4:14). His white hair represents Jesus as the Ancient of Days who will judge the living and the dead (Dan. 7:9-12 & Rev. 20:11-15). The God-man, who has suffered, now speaks to each of his churches.

All the churches that we are part of, will most likely be doing well in some areas and not so well in others. In each of the seven churches, Jesus complimented and rebuked them for what they were doing well and where repentance was needed. Since our churches belong to him, he himself is the best judge of our collective efforts.

When we gather together, do we look for this risen Jesus in our midst? Are we looking for the God-man Jesus to encourage and correct us? It can be too easy for us individually and as churches to only want to hear the encouragement and not the correction. Yet the correction, along with the encouragement, is also important.

Where we are strong, encouragement from Jesus will help us continue in the strength he highlights. If we have any sin, we need to repent, because otherwise, the consequences can be significant. This can include Jesus removing a church, as he threatens to do for the church in Ephesus (Rev. 2:4-5).

JESUS IN THE CHURCH

Some of Jesus' messages to the churches point out their great strengths and great weaknesses. We therefore cannot assume we are safe just because we have several strengths. These churches in Revelation had persevered through many hardships and persecutions, yet despite that, Jesus challenged them where needed.

Through John's writings, we see that Jesus was showing his churches his grace. He was giving them a chance to repent. It is far better for our mistakes and shortcomings to be pointed out by Jesus, so we get a chance to put them right before it is too late. His goal in all the letters was that they would listen, be victorious and receive their reward.

His commendations included patient endurance, of not tolerating wicked people, faithfulness to the point of death, and not renouncing faith, love, and righteousness, His rebukes included forsaking first love, idol sacrifice, sexual immorality, unfinished deeds, indifference and self-sufficiency.

Which of these rebukes apply to some of our churches today? If any of them do apply, we should heed Jesus's words:

> Those whom I love I rebuke and discipline. So be earnest and repent. Here I am! I stand at the door and knock. If anyone hears my voice and opens the door, I will come in and eat with that person, and they with me.
>
> Revelation 3:19-20.

This verse is often used in evangelism to represent Jesus knocking on the door of a sinner's heart, but the context is of Jesus knocking on the *door of a church*. Jesus was identifying issues that were affecting multiple people in the church. If we want to encounter Christ in the church, then we must respond to his encouragement and corrections.

This is our collective responsibility when we gather together. The Apostle Paul's instruction to us is "Let the message of Christ dwell among you richly as you teach and admonish one another with all wisdom through psalms, hymns, and songs from the Spirit" (Col. 3:16).

Can we pray for you?

The church service had finished and we were waiting in the queue to get a coffee. Ahead of us in the queue, was Matt who was a guest on our Alpha course. We asked Matt how his week had been. He said that he had been to the doctor to discuss blood treatments for Hepatitis C.

Matt was a recovering drug addict and he explained that the treatment would last either three or six months, depending on the result of the blood test that he would get the following week. We said to Matt, "Can we pray for you?", which he accepted. As we stood in the queue, we prayed that God would heal him and that he would not need any treatment at all.

At church a couple of weeks later, we saw Matt and he was beaming because his most recent blood test results had shown that he no longer had Hepatitis C! Matt was glad that he did not require any treatment because he was worried about some of the potential side effects. We celebrated with him in the miracle-working ability of Jesus.

When we had prayed for Matt, the church service had ended, the prayer ministry had finished and the worship band were packing away their instruments. Yet Jesus still was in his church, we found him right there in the coffee queue! Jesus loves to be among his people gathered together.

Do we look for Jesus when we are with our Christian brothers and sisters?

Reflection

Consider these verses:

> *But what about you?" he asked. 'Who do you say I am?"*
>
> *Simon Peter answered, 'You are the Messiah, the Son of the living God.'*
>
> *Jesus replied, 'Blessed are you, Simon son of Jonah, for this was not revealed to you by flesh and blood, but by my Father in heaven. And I tell you that you are Peter, and on this rock I will build my church, and the gates of Hades will not overcome it'.*
>
> Matthew 16:15-18

Ask Father God:

- Lord, do I consider church to be a building, meeting place or your people?
- Lord, am I open to your encouragement and correction?
- Lord, am I open and willing to talk about you to those around me who are not yet believers?

Prayer:

> *Thank you Father for giving us the Church. Help me to recognise when Jesus is present in my church*

gatherings. I pray that I will experience you in all the church activities and places they meet.

To do:

- Evaluate whether you expect Jesus to dwell in some or all of the different activities within your church.
- When you are next with other Christians, why not pray for a need that one of them may have and look for what Jesus does?
- When you are next with non-Christians, ask Jesus if he wants to speak to them through you.

Further reading:

- Matthew 18:15-19
- Acts 2:42-47
- 1 Corinthians 1:10-17

JESUS IN US

"Where is God? Where can I find him?" we ask. We don't realise that's like a fish swimming frantically through the ocean in search of the ocean.
(Ted Dekker, Author)

The Mystery of Christ

In the apostle Paul's letters, he describes a hidden mystery which is the secret will of God that has been hidden for ages and generations.[157] The apostle Peter tells us that the prophets and the angels searched intently and longed to understand this mystery (1 Pet. 1:10-12).

To understand the fullness of God we need to grasp the significance of this mystery. Paul says the riches of this mystery is "Christ in you, the hope of Glory" (Col. 1:27). Jesus said "Anyone who loves me will obey my teaching. My Father will love them, and we will come to them and make our home with them" (Jn. 14:23).

The God of the universe planned long ago that one day he would make his dwelling place in people – that is truly profound! There may be days that we doubt what God says or that he feels a million miles away, but the truth for Christians is that he is always within us. If we feel far from God, then that

---

[157] mystērion, Strong's G3466

feeling is misleading. We can't be geographically far from him if he is in us.

Why does God want to make his home in us? He changes us from the inside out so that we become *his* temple (1 Cor. 6:19-20). When we are born again, we are given God's seed so we will no longer be slaves to sin (Jn. 8:34-36). We also participate in God's divine nature and receive his power so that we have everything we need for a godly life (2 Pet. 1:3-9).

Having Christ in us means we will never be the same again. Our identity is changed so that we become children of God (Jn. 1:12-13). Author Joyce Meyer says, "The more we focus on who we are in Christ, the less it matters who we were in the past, or even what happened to us."[158] We are fundamentally different to what we were before we became a Christian.

Having Christ in us is not just about change within us, it is also so that we can introduce other people to Jesus. Paul tells us "When God, who set me apart from my mother's womb and called me by his grace, was pleased to reveal his Son in me so that I might preach him among the Gentiles." (Gal. 1:15-16).

Having God dwell in us means that he wants to reveal his Son to people around us. For Paul, it was the Gentiles and for Peter, it was the Jews (Gal. 2:8). With Christ in us, we are naturally evangelistic as his nature becomes our nature. Each of us is called by God to be his witness to people wherever we live and work (Acts 1:8).

The mystery of Christ is not just about Christ in an individual. This mystery is also that "through the gospel the Gentiles are heirs together with Israel, members together of one body, and

---

[158] Meyer, Joyce. *Beauty for Ashes: Receiving Emotional Healing*. FaithWords, 2003.

sharers together in the promise in Christ Jesus." (Eph. 3:6). Paul goes further and says there is no Gentile, Jew, male or female, as Jesus is all, and in all (Col. 3:11 & Gal. 3:26-29).

Again it is truly profound that those things that have brought injustice and conflict between people – such as gender, race, and ethnicity, no longer have to be an issue among God's people because we are now defined as children of God. Our old humanity died with

Jesus and we are new creations (2 Cor. 5:17) so that we can live and reign with him for eternity (2 Tim. 2:11-13).

> Have we truly grasped this mystery that we are part of? Paul says of Jesus:
>
> I keep asking that the God of our Lord Jesus Christ, the glorious Father, may give you the Spirit of wisdom and revelation, so that you may know him better.
>
> I pray that the eyes of your heart may be enlightened in order that you may know the hope to which he has called you, the riches of his glorious inheritance in his holy people, and his incomparably great power for us who believe.
>
> That power is the same as the mighty strength he exerted when he raised Christ from the dead and seated him at his right hand in the heavenly realms, far above all rule and authority, power and dominion, and every name that is invoked, not only in the present age but also in the one to come.
>
> And God placed all things under his feet and appointed him to be head over everything for the church, which

is his body, the fullness of him who fills everything in every way.

Ephesians 1:17-23

The fullness of God can be experienced when he fills us, a diverse multi-generational group of people. We now represent him because we are his children by adoption and also by experience (Eph. 1:4-5 & Rom. 5:5). Being a Christian transforms us individually, but being together as part of God's kingdom can transform the human race.

Do we underplay or downgrade the significance of Christ in us?

Despite these transformational truths about Christ in us, it is common to hear Christians say things like "I am looking forward to Sunday so that I can encounter God at church", or "The church building is God's house", and "I felt far from God yesterday, so I went to meet my friend to pray together".

Whilst there can be a greater collective experience of God when we gather as Christians, this does not diminish or reduce the significance of the truth that Christ is in us as individuals. Having a paradigm that the church building is the dwelling place of God rather than us is an Old Covenant perspective. God loves to meet with us as individuals or as a group whatever the geographical location.

Think about what Jesus said to the woman at a well in Samaria:

> 'Sir,' the woman said, 'I can see that you are a prophet. Our ancestors worshipped on this mountain, but you Jews claim that the place where we must worship is in Jerusalem.'

> 'Woman,' Jesus replied, 'believe me, a time is coming when you will worship the Father neither on this mountain nor in Jerusalem. You Samaritans worship what you do not know; we worship what we do know, for salvation is from the Jews. Yet a time is coming and has now come when the true worshippers will worship the Father in the Spirit and truth, for they are the kind of worshippers the Father seeks. God is spirit, and his worshippers must worship in the Spirit and truth.'
>
> John 4:19-24

These are some of the deepest truths about Christian worship that we find in the Bible and Jesus shares them with a Samaritan woman who has been marginalised by her community.[159] Such is the desire of God to rescue people from the margins of society so that they can know him and worship him!

Jesus says in these verses that Christian worship is not about *where* you worship, it is about *how* you worship. Yet liturgical worship services are still seen as the main activity within many churches across the world. There is importance in Christian communities coming together to worship, but this is not the be-all and end-all of worship.

This type of worship is typically sung worship, which is only one type of worship. One of the Hebrew words for worship means work, worship and service.[160] Therefore worship is about all of our lives; it is a lifestyle towards God. Worship is about how we work, how we relate to people and the decisions we make as well as when we do sung worship.

---

[159] We can deduce this because she comes to the well at noon, the hottest time of the day, when no one else would get water at this time.
[160] ābad, Strong's H5647

Since each one of us is the temple of the Holy Spirit, Christ in us affects all that we do. With God's power at work in us, he can do immeasurably more than we can ask or imagine (Eph. 3:20). Author Israelmore Ayivor says "What lies behind us may be mighty. What lies before us may be mightier. But what lies within us is the mightiest of all! Christ within us is the hope of Glory!"

Jesus said that the Father was in him and he was in the Father and that whatever the Father does, the Son also does (Jn. 14:20 & Jn. 5:19). Having Christ in us, and making his home in us, means that he influences us from the inside out. His passions, priorities and purposes should over time become ours.

Evangelist Kevin Dedmon says, "God wants you to have an encounter, so that you become an encounter, so that others can have an encounter!" Because we have Christ in us it means people around us can encounter Jesus – that means his love, his kingship and his miraculous power.

If we all had the same passion to encounter God in our everyday lives as we do to encounter God in a sung worship during a church meeting, the world would be a different place! Jesus saw what the Father was doing and joined in, which is what we can learn to do. With Christ in us, we should also join in with what the Father is doing.

If we meet people who are feeling hopeless, fearful, or confused, we can pray for them to receive God's hope, peace and joy. We can bring the kingdom of God into people's situations around us. When people meet us they can meet Christ in us. Grasping the significance that God makes his home in us is a game-changer as to how we live our lives.

Christ in us is a guarantee of our salvation

Do you ever have a day when you wonder if you are a Christian? If so, you will not be the only person that sometimes has a day like that. There are moments in our lives that can be hard, confusing and painful. Yet our circumstances do not dictate whether we are saved or not. Christ in us helps us know our salvation is real.

In Paul's letter to the Ephesians, he helps them understand the significance of what it means to have Christ in us:

> In him we were also chosen, having been predestined according to the plan of him who works out everything in conformity with the purpose of his will, in order that we, who were the first to put our hope in Christ, might be for the praise of his glory. And you also were included in Christ when you heard the message of truth, the gospel of your salvation.
>
> When you believed, you were marked in him with a seal, the promised Holy Spirit, who is a deposit guaranteeing our inheritance until the redemption of those who are God's possession – to the praise of his glory.
>
> Ephesians 1:11-14

When we receive the Holy Spirit in us he is a seal, deposit and guarantee of our inheritance and place in heaven for eternity. "Seal" means to mark a person as belonging to God and to authenticate beyond doubt our profession to Christ.[161] This

---

[161] sphragizō. Strong's G4972

language is similar to legal language, meaning it would remain uncontested if taken to court.

The deposit is a pledge or downpayment where the full amount will be subsequently paid.[162] Receiving the Holy Spirit is proof to us that our salvation is real, even though we won't fully experience it until Jesus comes again. God wants us to exercise faith in his promises.

Whenever we hear his voice, understand a scripture, feel his comfort, and experience an answered prayer – these are all assurances that we are Christians. Paul says that we belong to him, that we are his possession, his property. He has purchased us through his death on the cross (Gal. 3:13).

Paul also underlines this truth, when he writes to the church in Corinth:

> For no matter how many promises God has made, they are 'Yes' in Christ. And so through him the 'Amen' is spoken by us to the glory of God. Now it is God who makes both us and you stand firm in Christ. He anointed us, set his seal of ownership on us, and put his Spirit in our hearts as a deposit, guaranteeing what is to come.
>
> 2 Cor. 1:20-22

Having been anointed in the Holy Spirit means that we belong to him and this promise has an unbreakable 'Yes' in Christ. Therefore any feelings or doubts that suggest the opposite are misleading and untrue. Jesus' death and resurrection are unshakable truths that define our salvation.

---

[162] arrabōn, Strong's G728

When we have feelings or doubts that suggest we do not belong to Jesus, we need to meditate on the Biblical truths. We can also ask Christ in us why we may be struggling to believe them, which may be because our upbringing or circumstances have led us to find it hard to trust people. It also may be because we are more aware of our sin than anything else in that moment.

We need to educate our thoughts and feelings to be in line with the reality of who Jesus is and who we are in him. We have the ability to change how we think and feel by increasing our understanding of our thoughts and behaviours. These give us the insight we need to make positive changes in our lives.[163]

As well as prayer and encouragement from others, many practical tools can be helpful to analyse and change our thoughts and behaviours.[164] Our life experiences can give us negative biases in our thoughts, feelings and self-esteem. For deep-rooted issues, you may want to consider a combination of prayer and therapy or counselling.

Christ in us helps us to resist temptation

Jesus had many significant moments when he was alone, away from his disciples. When we are alone, it can feel like there is no one to help us – yet this is far from true if Christ is in us. Jesus models to us many moments when he was alone which he confidently embraced because he knew his Father was always with him.

---

[163] BetterHelp Editorial Team. "Can People Change, Or Do They Just Lie? Understanding Personal Growth". *BetterHelp*. https://www.betterhelp.com/advice/behavior/can-people-change-or-do-they-just-lie

[164] GetSelfHelp. "Free Downloads 2 - CBT Worksheets". *GetSelfHelp*, https://www.getselfhelp.co.uk/free-downloads-2-cbt-worksheets

One of these moments was when Jesus was led by the Spirit into the wilderness to be tested:

> Jesus, full of the Holy Spirit, left the Jordan and was led by the Spirit into the wilderness, where for forty days he was tempted by the devil. He ate nothing during those days, and at the end of them he was hungry.
> The devil said to him, 'If you are the Son of God, tell this stone to become bread.'
>
> Jesus answered, 'It is written: "Man shall not live on bread alone."'
>
> The devil led him up to a high place and showed him in an instant all the kingdoms of the world. And he said to him, 'I will give you all their authority and splendour; it has been given to me, and I can give it to anyone I want to. If you worship me, it will all be yours.'
>
> Jesus answered, 'It is written: "Worship the Lord your God and serve him only."'
>
> The devil led him to Jerusalem and had him stand on the highest point of the temple. 'If you are the Son of God,' he said, 'throw yourself down from here. For it is written:
>
> '"He will command his angels concerning you to guard you carefully; they will lift you up in their hands, so that you will not strike your foot against a stone."'
>
> Jesus answered, 'It is said: "Do not put the Lord your God to the test."'

> When the devil had finished all this tempting, he left him until an opportune time.
>
> Luke 4:1-13

In the wilderness, Jesus was not by himself, he would have known that his Father was with him[165]. Despite being hungry, he resisted Satan three times and did not bow to him or his temptations. These temptations were potentially about identity, basic needs, misuse of power, riches, protection and who we worship, all of which we are likely to be tempted by.

When we are being tempted, what is our perspective? Is it, like Jesus, that God is able to meet our needs and we do not need to find them elsewhere? Is it that our relationship with him is enough and that we don't need recognition from anyone else? It is that we will trust him with his timing and not look for shortcuts to the promises he has made?

At times when we are tempted and tested, we, like Jesus, can quote the truth of the scripture to encourage us to keep true to God. Yet often we can feel alone in such moments, as if God may have abandoned us. This is not the case because we have Christ in us, the one who overcame his temptations.

Jesus is not just an example to us, he is now within us and so can empower us to overcome all temptation:

> For this reason he had to be made like them, fully human in every way, in order that he might become a merciful and faithful high priest in service to God, and that he might make atonement for the sins of the people.

---

[165] Biblically, the wilderness was a place where people encountered God, not a place void of God. Many of the Old Testament patriarchs met God in the wilderness.

> Because he himself suffered when he was tempted, he is able to help those who are being tempted.
>
> Hebrews 2:17-18

Even when temptations can feel so appealing or inescapable, he can help us say 'no' to them. His inward strength can become ours as we seek him. We do not need to fear temptation because "God is our refuge and strength, an ever-present help in trouble." (Psalm 46:1).

There are practical things we can do to help us not give in to temptation. Pray, go for a walk to clear your head, remove yourself from the tempting situation or contact a Christian friend for encouragement. Worship and prayer help us focus on God's love for us. Jesus says that the Spirit is willing to do the right thing but our mind and body at times are not (Mt. 26:41-42).

The more we say 'yes' to God and 'no' to the body will result in a growing strength to resist temptations. If we do fall into temptation we need to avoid self-condemnation – another unhelpful thought and feeling which may take us on a downward spiral into feeling we are a failure and can sap us of strength to do the right thing.

Jesus forgives all our sins, so if we fall into temptation we go back to him and seek forgiveness. His kindness leads to repentance (Rom. 2:4). Jesus' love and kindness towards us is a great motivator to shape our lives to how Jesus wants them to be. One of his priorities for us is that we know we are loved and forgiven and know how to live righteously.

Christ in us helps us pray

We are invited into a vibrant prayer life. Jesus gave us a template for prayer, which we call the Lord's Prayer, but more importantly, we have the one in us who knows how to pray. The best way to learn how to pray is to follow Jesus' example in the Bible and how the Spirit wants to intercede through us.

> We know that the whole creation has been groaning as in the pains of childbirth right up to the present time. Not only so, but we ourselves, who have the firstfruits of the Spirit, groan inwardly as we wait eagerly for our adoption to sonship, the redemption of our bodies. For in this hope we were saved. But hope that is seen is no hope at all. Who hopes for what they already have? But if we hope for what we do not yet have, we wait for it patiently.
>
> In the same way, the Spirit helps us in our weakness. We do not know what we ought to pray for, but the Spirit himself intercedes for us through wordless groans. And he who searches our hearts knows the mind of the Spirit, because the Spirit intercedes for God's people in accordance with the will of God.
>
> And we know that in all things God works for the good of those who love him, who have been called according to his purpose. For those God foreknew he also predestined to be conformed to the image of his Son, that he might be the firstborn among many brothers and sisters. And those he predestined, he also called; those he called, he also justified; those he justified, he also glorified.
>
> Romans 8:22-30

When we pray we cannot be alone because we have Christ in us, the one who knows how to pray to the Father. Jesus often withdrew so he could spend time with his Father and pray.[166] Jesus made it his practice to pray in a solitary place and he also sought out his Father when he felt overwhelmed. Sometimes he prayed early in the morning and at other times at night.

How is your prayer life? Are you getting away from the distractions of modern life to be with your heavenly Father? Are you learning to pray through the Spirit when you do not know what to pray? Is Christ in you creating yearnings to see more of God in your own life and the lives of others?

As we spend time in prayer, it allows Jesus to shape our passions and desires so that they align with his. Jesus wants to mould us so that we think, speak and act like him and spending time in personal prayer is a key way for this to happen. Letting Him pray through us allows us to feel his heart and know his will.

Setting aside a regular time to pray and fast can help to make it a lifestyle. Sometimes it is helpful just to worship and encounter Jesus, at other times it is good to pray for people and situations. All good practices require some perseverance to enable them to become a regular and a normal part of our lives.

As Paul says, sometimes we do not know how to pray for a person or situation, but Jesus always does. In these moments we need to look to the Holy Spirit for how to pray even if that results in longings and groans, some of which we may not understand. God knows his will for situations and people, which at times he may share with us.

---

[166] For example, Mt. 14:13, Mk. 1:35, Mk. 6:45-46, Mk. 14:32-34, Lk. 4:42, Lk. 5:16, Lk. 6:12, Lk. 9:18 and Jn. 6:15

God invites us into the process of his will becoming manifest on earth. Prayer and fasting are part of how this happens, so it is helpful to see this as a privilege rather than a burden. Make time when you pray to ask Jesus what is on his heart and mind so that Christ in you can lead you in prayer.

It can be helpful to keep a prayer journal so that you can record what you prayed. It may not need to be very detailed but to record simply the person and situation you prayed for. You can then review how your prayers are being answered, which will build faith and your confidence in God, who works for the good of those who love him.

Some of this may be familiar if you have been a Christian for any length of time, but have we let the basics fall by the wayside in the busyness of life?

Christ in us helps us share our faith

We were asked at a conference session we were speaking at by one of the attendees how they could share their faith with others when they were the only Christian there at that moment, as they found such situations difficult. Doing evangelism together has many benefits because we can encourage each other, but there will be evangelistic moments when we are on our own.

We made the point that we are never alone in an evangelistic moment because we have Christ in us. Christ in us can give us courage and wisdom during such moments. Jesus was sometimes on his own when he shared the kingdom. For example, Jesus was on his own with the Samaritan woman at a well, yet knew his Father was with him (Jn. 4:1-26).

As evangelists, we often have people say to us that they wished we were there to help them with an evangelistic moment with a friend or work colleague. We know why they say this because they perceive we would be helpful to them during this moment, despite the fact they have Christ in them.

The likely truth is that they are the best person for that moment as God has orchestrated it. The testimony of the work that God has done in them up to this point is most likely what the non-Christian needs to hear because it will be relevant to them. God can create an evangelistic moment tailor-made for both the Christian and non-Christian.

During one of our DASEL evangelistic training courses, one of the attendees, Dave, was sharing with the group how he was renewing his car insurance; he had been involved in a serious road accident the previous year. Dave was grateful for God's faithfulness through this difficult year.

That week, whilst Dave was speaking with his insurance agent, they got chatting and Dave got to explain to the agent that he had been involved in a head-on car crash. The insurance agent replied by saying his sister-in-law also had a nasty car accident about the same time. Dave shared how God had been with him and sustained him through this whole process and brought healing at numerous junctures.

Maybe at this moment, when he heard Dave's story, the insurance agent was concerned about his sister-in-law. Only God would be able to orchestrate such an evangelistic moment, taking such a personal story and making it relevant to a non-Christian. We often hear similar stories from attendees of the DASEL Course.[167]

---

[167] Evangelism Reimagined. "The DASEL Course". *Evangelism Reimagined.* https://www.evangelismreimagined.org/dasel

This is what life is like when we recognise that we have Christ in us. Sharing our faith can become an exciting adventure as we link how God is working in us, to how he wants to work through us to other people. We have his power to pray for people and see them healed.

Jesus' instructions to his disciples, when they went to unbelievers, were simple:

> When you enter a house, first say, "Peace to this house." If someone who promotes peace is there, your peace will rest on them; if not, it will return to you. Stay there, eating and drinking whatever they give you, for the worker deserves his wages. Do not move around from house to house.
>
> When you enter a town and are welcomed, eat what is offered to you. Heal those there who are ill and tell them, "The kingdom of God has come near to you."
>
> Luke 10:5-9

Because we have Christ in us, these instructions are not complicated We can rely solely on his ability to work in and through us to reach the people around us. We can be confident that God has chosen the times and places where they would be born so that they seek God out and find him. We can partner with him as we confidently allow him to work through us (Acts 17:26-27).

Christ in us enables miracles to happen

One of the ways that Jesus shows he is King is through his miracles. He also chooses to do miracles through us. God testifies to the great salvation that we are part of by signs, wonders, miracles and gifts of the Holy Spirit (Heb. 2:4). We are also enabled by God to perform miracles (Acts 14:3).

Jesus' instructions to his apostles were as follows:

> Jesus called his twelve disciples to him and gave them authority to drive out impure spirits and to heal every disease and illness.
>
> As you go, proclaim this message: "The kingdom of heaven has come near." Heal those who are ill, raise the dead, cleanse those who have leprosy, drive out demons. Freely you have received; freely give.
>
> Matthew 10:1 & 7

When our children were school-age, Fiona met many other mums at the school gate. One of their husbands had recently died of a heart attack, leaving her and three children. This woman had a degenerative back condition and Fiona suggested that we go to pray for her.

Even though I did not know her well, I decided to go around to her house and offer to pray for her. I placed my hand on her back and prayed for her back to be healed. Nothing seemed to happen at that moment, but we did have a conversation about God and I invited her to the Alpha Course that Fiona and I were running at our church.

A few days later she communicated to us that her back was completely healed and she no longer needed her walking stick. She also said that she had reported to the local government that she no longer needed disability benefits, but they struggled to process this request because it was out of the ordinary!

This woman then came to the Alpha Course and became a Christian because she knew God was real. All she needed to do was to find out what he was like and whether he was worth following for the rest of her life. This experience grew our faith to pray for miraculous healing more often.

On subsequent Alpha Courses, we would make it our practice to pray for guests after the talk "Does God Heal Today?". Before the event, we would ask God for prophetic words and display them on a screen. We would then ask the guests whether any of them were relevant. Many of the guests were healed by Jesus.

We would encourage you to pray for people that you meet who need healing or a miracle. When we do this, we gently ask them if they would like to be prayed for and then simply ask Jesus to come and heal them. Christ in you is *the* miracle worker, let him work in and through you to heal others.

Christ in us the hope of glory

Christ in us is the hidden mystery that has now been made known. It is our hope of glory that can transform our and others' experience of God (Col. 1:27). We are far from powerless in our Christian lives when we recognise and embrace this truth. God is in you which means that he can empower your prayers and evangelism.

To be all that God want us to be requires us to recognise the significance of Christ in us, and know that we are never alone because the Trinity has made their home in us. As theologian Dietrich Bonhoeffer said, "God loves the world ...not an ideal world, but the real world" and therefore also said, "I need the Christ that is in you, and you need the Christ that is in me."

The apostle Paul puts it like this: "I have been crucified with Christ and I no longer live, but Christ lives in me. The life I now live in the body, I live by faith in the Son of God, who loved me and gave himself for me." (Gal. 2:20). With Christ in you, your life can be far from ordinary!

Will we make time to discover the riches of Christ within us?

Reflection

Consider these verses:

> *'If you love me, keep my commands. And I will ask the Father, and he will give you another advocate to help you and be with you for ever – the Spirit of truth. The world cannot accept him, because it neither sees him nor knows him. But you know him, for he lives with you and will be in you. I will not leave you as orphans; I will come to you.*
>
> *Before long, the world will not see me any more, but you will see me. Because I live, you also will live. On that day you will realise that I am in my Father, and you are in me, and I am in you. Whoever has my commands and keeps them is the one who loves me. The one who loves me will be loved by my Father, and I too will love them and show myself to them.'*
>
> *Then Judas (not Judas Iscariot) said, 'But, Lord, why do you intend to show yourself to us and not to the world?'*
>
> *Jesus replied, 'Anyone who loves me will obey my teaching. My Father will love them, and we will come to them and make our home with them'.*
>
> John 14:15-23

Ask Father God:

- Lord, have I got any areas of my life where I feel like an orphan?
- Lord, how can I be more intentional about praying and resisting temptation?

- Lord, who do I know that is unwell that you would like me to pray for to be healed?

Prayer:

> *Thank you for making your home in me. Help me fully grasp what it means to have Christ in me and that I am never alone. Show me how to impact others with your life-changing power that is within me.*

To do:

- Create a lifestyle of prayer for your life and the lives of others. What times of day and different durations work for you?
- If you are struggling with a specific temptation, why not ask a trusted Christian friend or church minister to help you get free?
- Each day ask Jesus how he wants to work in and through you.

Further reading:

- Matthew 6:5-13
- 1 Corinthians 10:11-14
- 2 Corinthians 4:1-18

JESUS AMONG THE LOST

*"My message is always the same;
it's how to get us sure enough of God's love, so we can
go out and share it with the lost."*
(Jackie Pullinger, Missionary & Author)

Why did Jesus come?

Simon Sinek is an author and inspirational speaker. His book *Start with Why* is a New York Times bestseller and his TED Talks on the concept of *why* have reached over 100 million around the world. He says we can achieve more if we start with everything we do by first asking "Why?".

Asking ourselves why we do something helps explain what we do, it gives us purpose and reason for being. "Why" also fuels our motivation to be a better person and the impetus to change the world around us. Understanding the "why" gives our lives meaning and contributes to the right motivation for sharing our faith.

Jesus has a "why".

His "why" is the biggest "why" there is, and if we choose to follow him, then his "why" will become our "why". If we want more of God in our lives, Jesus' "why" will have pre-eminence in our lives through our priorities. Understanding why Jesus came provides us with the meaning of why we have been sent (Lk. 9:1-6 and Lk. 10:1-7).

Jesus' "why" defines who we are, what we should do and how we should do it. His "why" is what shapes our core being and identity. It defines our chief purpose and the reason why we are not teleported to heaven the moment we become Christians! Jesus' "why" gives all our individual salvation stories significance.

Jesus' "why" is the most important, significant and fulfilling cause in the universe, in which he invites all of us to take part. His "Plan A" to fulfil this is to involve us; it is the greatest privilege we will ever receive. Jesus is personally inviting all of us to help him fulfil it, we all have a unique place in his plan.

So what is Jesus' "why"? Why did Jesus come? What is so important to Jesus?

> For the Son of Man came to seek and to save the lost.
>
> Luke 19:10

> 'It is not the healthy who need a doctor, but those who are ill. But go and learn what this means: "I desire mercy, not sacrifice." For I have not come to call the righteous, but sinners.'
>
> Matthew 9:12-13

> Jesus replied, 'Let us go somewhere else – to the nearby villages – so that I can preach there also. That is why I have come.'

> So he travelled throughout Galilee, preaching in their synagogues and driving out demons.
>
> Mark 1:38-39

> I have come that they may have life, and have it to the full.
>
> John 10:10

> Now this is eternal life: that they know you, the only true God, and Jesus Christ, whom you have sent. Righteous Father ... I have made you known.
>
> John 17:3, 25-26

Jesus' "why", the reason he came, is to reconcile sinners to the Father.

He did not stay in the same place because there were always others who needed to experience his kingdom and hear his invitation. He invites us to do the same, which is what we commonly refer to as the Great Commission:

> Then Jesus came to them and said, 'All authority in heaven and on earth has been given to me. Therefore go and make disciples of all nations, baptising them in the name of the Father and of the Son and of the Holy Spirit, and teaching them to obey everything I have commanded you. And surely I am with you always, to the very end of the age.'
>
> Matthew 28:18-20

An important priority

Seeking and saving the lost was, and still is, a priority for Jesus. He does not think about the needs of the lost only after the needs of the church have been taken care of. Jesus would regularly allow his agenda to be interrupted if there was an unbeliever his Father wanted him to speak with.

There is also a significant amount of space in the gospels that records Jesus speaking to the lost, both individually and with crowds. Stories of men and women coming to faith are recorded in the gospels for our encouragement. Jesus drew people from all parts of society to himself.

Think about how Nathanael comes to faith when Jesus said he saw him under a fig tree (John 1:45-51). Think about Mary, who came to faith through Jesus's friendship, comfort and miraculous raising of her dead brother (John 11:1-46). Think about Zacchaeus the despised tax collector, who comes to faith because Jesus treated him with compassion, dignity and kindness (Luke 19:1-10).

These people had unique stories and encounters with Jesus. When the lost had an experience of Jesus, their lives changed. The same can be true of us since we have Christ within us. We get to introduce Jesus to unbelievers around us. We do this so that people can discover who he is and what he is like before they can put their faith in him.

Why does Jesus include us?

Pause for a moment.

What emotion does it evoke when you read the words "Great Commission"? Is it a positive one or a negative one? The word 'great' can be defined in multiple ways – magnitude, pre-eminence, eminence, nobility and enthusiasm.[168] We do not know who coined the term *Great Commission*, but its aims were seen positively by missionaries such as Hudson Taylor.

If you have a negative emotion associated with the Great Commission or evangelism, you are not alone. Large numbers of Christians have disengaged from evangelism, having struggled with, or had bad experiences with using evangelistic methods. It is estimated that 80 percent of all Western Christians do not consistently witness for Christ.[169]

Sadly, throughout church history, Jesus' "why" has often been ignored or replaced by a lesser mission and purpose. Many Christians struggle or discount themselves from joining Jesus in his "why". Over the twenty-five years we have been teaching and training churches in evangelism, we find this is all too common.

This reality is far from God's intent, he *wants us* to partner with him to bring about the Great Commission. His personal invitation to each of us is the greatest invitation we will ever receive. You can freely enjoy sharing your faith. In fact, it can become your greatest adventure.

If you have struggled with or had negative experiences of evangelism, they do not need to define your norm. When Jesus sent out his disciples to do evangelism they returned with joy (Lk. 10:17). This is how Jesus intends us to experience the Great Commission. Yes, it can be hard work and requires sacrifice, but it also comes with joy!

---

[168] Merriam-Webster. https://www.merriam-webster.com/dictionary/great
[169] Gilpin, Mark & Fiona. "Do you struggle with evangelism? You are not alone". *Evangelism Reimagined*, https://www.evangelismreimagined.org/do-you-struggle-with-evangelism-you-are-not-alone

So why does Jesus invite us to take part? He does this because the way he works in our lives can be a powerful testimony to people just like us and to people who have had similar experiences to you. Your stories of answered prayers, miraculous healing and provision, and your hope and joy can influence others to choose Jesus.

We should never discount ourselves or the work of God in us. We are living and breathing examples of what it looks like to have God's Kingdom come into our lives. Within the complexity and mess of the world we live in, people around us are looking for answers. As God works in us, we become a powerful advert for him.

It is God's choice to involve us in the Great Commission, so it is important to ask whether we believe in his plan. If God has chosen to work through us then it is the best plan there is, because he is the wisest being in the universe. God has not made a mistake to involve us in his plan, it is actually a genius move.

By working in and through Christians across the globe, Jesus can continually impact countless people at any one moment. He can also put us in the path of people who will relate to our specific testimony because it will be relevant to them. Having confidence in God's ability to use us is key to enjoying and being fruitful in evangelism.

If you want to discover God's solutions for hindrances to evangelism and sharing our faith, we explore these in further detail with our book *God's Dream Our Greatest Privilege*[170]. Evangelism does not need to be a struggle or a chore. You can be set free from any fear and hindrances and freely enjoy sharing your faith.

---

[170] Evangelism Reimagined Books. https://www.evangelismreimagined.org/books

The importance of Pentecost

One of Jesus' key priorities was to seek and save the lost. He also invited his disciples to join him in this task; first the twelve disciples who were sent to the Jews, and then the seventy disciples who were sent to the Gentiles (Mt. 10:1 & Lk. 10:1). These two sending moments represented sending his disciples to all people of the known world.

When Jesus first appeared to his disciples after his resurrection, he said "As the Father has sent me, I am sending you.' And with that he breathed on them and said, 'Receive the Holy Spirit." (Jn. 20:21-22). Before he ascended to heaven he gave the disciples his mission to make disciples (Mt. 28:16-20).

At Pentecost, the Holy Spirit came powerfully on the gathered disciples:

> When the day of Pentecost came, they were all together in one place. Suddenly a sound like the blowing of a violent wind came from heaven and filled the whole house where they were sitting. They saw what seemed to be tongues of fire that separated and came to rest on each of them. All of them were filled with the Holy Spirit and began to speak in other tongues as the Spirit enabled them.
>
> Acts 2:1-4

It is important to grasp the significance of this event for two reasons. Firstly, in the time leading up to Jesus, the presence of God was usually only encountered by a few select individuals for a specific task and a high priest. It was a sign that God had come to live among his people. At the dedication of the first temple built by Solomon, the presence of God came as a cloud and filled the temple (2 Chronicles 5:13-14).

Yet at Pentecost, the Holy Spirit came and filled *people*, not a building. It was like God left the temple building and people became his home (Eph. 3:16-19). His filling of people was a public spectacle in front of God-fearing Jews from every nation. Peter then stands to explain to his fellow Jews what this recent event meant.

This resulted in over 3000 people being saved. At the time of Jesus, the population of Jerusalem was about 25,000[171], but during festival times could be somewhere near 100,000.[172] In this profound moment, 3 percent of the current population of Jerusalem become Christians. This moment had a significant impact on those in Jerusalem.

Do you realise that the first fruits of the disciples being baptised in the Holy Spirit were evangelistic? This was not by chance. The Jews also celebrated the Feast of Firstfruits alongside Pentecost (Lev. 23:4-8). The Feast of Firstfruits marked thanksgiving to God for the first fruits of the harvest.

There were fifty days between these feasts and also fifty days between Jesus' death and the giving of the Holy Spirit at Pentecost. This makes a powerful statement that those who were born again and baptised by the Holy Spirit at Pentecost are just the first fruits of a worldwide multigenerational harvest.

---

[171] Jackson, Wayne, "How Many People Were in Jerusalem When Jesus Was Crucified?". Christian Courier. https://christiancourier.com/articles/how-many-people-were-in-jerusalem-when-jesus-was-crucified

[172] Van Biema, David. "Jerusalem At the Time of Jesus". *Time*. https://content.time.com/time/subscriber/article/0,33009,999673-1,00.html

This was just the beginning of Jesus' inheritance of the "great multitude that no one could count, from every nation, tribe, people and language, standing before the throne and before the Lamb." (Rev. 7:9). One of the main reasons we are baptised in the Holy Spirit is to make us evangelistic, yet this truth seems to escape many Christians.

This aligns with how Jesus sent out his disciples. We are to take the presence of God and his kingdom to wherever people are. Jesus' mission strategy is for us to be filled with the Holy Spirit and live like we are sent to people. This could be either to an unreached people group or, for most of us, to the people we live and work amongst.

This is a very simple strategy – God indwells people all over the world, so he can reach the maximum number possible – it is genius! God wants us to partner with him in our everyday life, where we are, doing what we do, and being ourselves so that people can encounter him where they are.

Do we recognise that Jesus is putting us at the centre of his plan intentionally, purposefully and joyfully? Have we grasped that God in us is a powerful missional influence? Do we therefore joyfully join in with what God is already doing in the lives of unbelievers around us (Jn. 16:8-11)?

There is no better plan, but do we believe in Jesus' plan?

The workers are few

Despite this simple and ingenious strategy, the majority of Western Christians do not join in Jesus' mission. Many do not realise that Jesus has put us at the centre of his strategy. He has chosen us all to be his labourers in the ripe harvest fields (Jn. 4:35). We are to join him there and work alongside him.

Most of Jesus' teachings on prayer were about *how* to pray. There are only a few examples of things he said to pray and ask for.[173] So we can safely conclude that when Jesus says there is something to ask or pray for, it is important. So when Jesus asks us to pray for workers, it is because it is central to his harvest strategy.

> Jesus went through all the towns and villages, teaching in their synagogues, proclaiming the good news of the kingdom and healing every disease and illness. When he saw the crowds, he had compassion on them, because they were harassed and helpless, like sheep without a shepherd.
>
> Then he said to his disciples, 'The harvest is plentiful but the workers are few. Ask the Lord of the harvest, therefore, to send out workers into his harvest field.' Jesus called his twelve disciples to him and gave them authority to drive out impure spirits and to heal every disease and illness.
>
> Matthew 9:35–10:1

Despite this specific request by Jesus for us to pray for harvest workers, think about all the times you have prayed with others – how often have you heard such a prayer? In this passage, when Jesus speaks about sending out workers, it means to compel in haste, in rapid motion to move straight towards its intended goal.[174] This suggests there is no room for ambiguity, delay or distraction.

---

[173] Examples include Mt. 5:44 and Mk. 14:38
[174] ekballō, Strong's G1544

For Jesus' strategy to work, it means churches are required to spend significant effort creating and developing harvest workers who share Jesus' priority and resilience to seek and save the lost. Without harvest workers, the ripe fields cannot be harvested and therefore fewer people are likely to become Christians.

Research statistics about harvest workers are not very encouraging. The London Institute for Contemporary Christianity research shows that 98% of Christians are neither envisioned nor equipped for mission in 95% of their waking lives.[175] They conclude "The sacred-secular divide is the malignant foe of fruitful mission and joyful Christian living across the globe."

The Jesus Film Project's multigenerational survey on evangelism shows that despite 70% of survey respondents agreeing that it is very important to share their faith, only about 13% regularly talk about spiritual matters with people who voice beliefs they would disagree with. 12% of survey respondents rarely or never shared their faith.[176]

When asked what prevented them from sharing their faith, the five top answers were 1. fear (22%), 2. lack of opportunity (17%), 3. nothing (17%), 4. unequipped (10%) and 5. lack of interest (10%). Other issues were busyness, shyness, not finding it easy, and not wanting to come across as pushy or offensive.[177]

When asked which ministries were most important out of church planting, translation, humanitarian aid, direct evangelism and equipping people to share, nearly one out of

---

[175] Greene, Mark. "The Great Divide". *LICC.* https://licc.org.uk/resources/the-great-divide
[176] Jesus Film Project. "Jesus Film Project's Multigenerational Survey on Evangelism". *Jesus Film Project.* https://www.jesusfilm.org/blog/jfp-multigenerational-survey-evangelism
[177] Jesus Film Project. "We Asked 1,600+ Christians Why They Don't Share Their Faith". *Jesus Film Project.* https://www.jesusfilm.org/blog/christian-evangelism-statistics

every three (32%) respondents suggested that equipping people to share the gospel was their top priority.

A survey in the UK by the Evangelical Alliance found that a third of individuals (34%) said their church wasn't helping them with evangelism at all, and only 13% of individuals said their church regularly helped with evangelism. It also found that only 12% of respondents invited someone to Alpha or a similar course.[178]

These statistics highlight significant issues for the Western church, the most important being that there are not enough harvest workers and this has resulted in a decline in Christianity. Contrary to this is the growth of Christianity in Africa, Asia and Latin America, whose churches generally put a greater emphasis on evangelism and mission.[179]

There also seems to be a disconnect between Christians saying that being equipped to share their faith is important and that some of their churches are not helping them with their evangelism. Also, a greater percentage of younger Christians think it is wrong to share their personal beliefs with someone of a different faith in the hope that they will convert.[180]

To give an analogous illustration, during World War II, most men aged 18-41 were conscripted into the armed services. 10% of all male conscripts aged 18–25 performed vital and dangerous civil conscription service in coal mines.[181] Almost

---

[178] EAUK. "Changing Church Autumn Survey". *EAUK.*
https://www.eauk.org/assets/files/downloads/Changing-church-autumn-survey-disicipleship-evangelism-and-community-engagement.pdf
[179] OC Research. "Africa's Amazing Christian Growth". *OC Research.*
https://www.ocresearch.info/?q=content/africa%E2%80%99s-amazing-christian-growth
[180] Barna Group. "Almost Half of Practicing Christian Millennials Say Evangelism Is Wrong". *Barna.* https://www.barna.com/research/millennials-oppose-evangelism
[181] Find My Past. "The Bevin Boys: Conscripts for the Mines". *Find My Past.*
https://www.findmypast.co.uk/1939register/the-bevin-boys

90% of single women and 80% of married women were working in factories, on the land or in the armed forces.[182]

During World War II there was a willingness in the nation for both men and women in the UK to volunteer for service. Today, during peacetime, the UK has approx. 190 thousand service personnel, which equates to about 1.2% of people that could be conscripted. With so few harvest workers in the field, does the UK church erroneously have a peacetime mentality?

Within the UK church, it now seems the norm for most church members not to regularly engage in the Great Commission. In comparison to World War II, it is like volunteering and conscription has been reversed with the majority staying at home. Is the need to save souls so that Jesus can deservedly gain his inheritance a lesser cause than World War II (Ps. 2:7-8)?

When employers are looking for staff they typically look for qualities such as reliability, dedication, team player, good communication, willingness to learn, and integrity. Would it not be the case that such qualities would describe many Christians? So if this is what Jesus is looking for in a worker, why would most Christians not feel able to take part in the harvest?

Not only that, but ministry has become something that is predominantly defined *within* the church walls. Whilst ministry has a place within the church, a significant part of the ministry of Jesus and the apostles was among the unsaved. Biblically speaking, the ministry that has been given to us all is the ministry of reconciliation.

---

[182] UK Government. "The women of the Second World War". *GOV.UK.*
https://www.gov.uk/government/news/the-women-of-the-second-world-war

> All this is from God, who reconciled us to himself through Christ and gave us the ministry of reconciliation: that God was reconciling the world to himself in Christ, not counting people's sins against them.
>
> And he has committed to us the message of reconciliation. We are therefore Christ's ambassadors, as though God were making his appeal through us. We implore you on Christ's behalf: Be reconciled to God.
>
> 2 Corinthians 5:18-20

The letter that Paul wrote to the church in Corinth was read publicly for all to hear and also in other churches (Col. 4:16). This privilege of this ministry is given to *all of us*; Paul did not consider it optional. In this passage, Paul is helping us understand that our collective Christian identity and calling is rooted in God making his appeal through us.

So any apostolic, prophetic, teaching, pastoral or evangelistic ministry should serve the greater mandate of reconciling the world to Jesus. If any ministry is disconnected from this collective calling, it is in danger of not being aligned with God's priorities. The evangelists' role is to equip others to take part in this mandate; they are not meant to be the only workers in the harvest fields on behalf of other Christians (Eph. 4:11-13)!

Is the gospel still relevant today?

Whilst church attendance has been declining in Western society, globally it is a different story.[183] The number of

---

[183] Churchtrac. "The State of Church Attendance: Trends and Statistics [2024]". *Churchtrac*. https://www.churchtrac.com/articles/the-state-of-church-attendance-trends-and-statistics-2023

Christians has significantly grown in the last century, from about 600 million to more than 2 billion.[184] The gospel continues to change people's lives all across the world, particularly in sub-Saharan Africa and the Asia-Pacific region.

There are also encouraging stories within Western society. The Alpha Course is one of these. It started in 1977 at Holy Trinity Brompton and by 1998 10,500 courses were being run.[185] More than 28 million people have now attended the course worldwide, nearly 5 million in the UK, and many have become Christians as a result.[186]

In 2016, Alpha International conducted a global study on the impact of Alpha across 11 countries. It found that since doing Alpha, 82% of non-Christian attendees described themselves as followers of Jesus. 93% of churches said Alpha was an effective tool for evangelism.[187]

During the 1904–1905 Welsh Revival, 100,000 people were saved.[188] The population of Wales at that time was approximately 2 million, meaning that 5% of the population was saved. Comparing this to the 5 million people in the UK that have attended Alpha as of 2022, it equates to 7 percent of the UK population at the time.[189]

Not all of these people who attended Alpha Courses will have been saved, but using the 82% non-Christian attendees statistic

---

[184] Pew Research Center. "Global Christianity – A Report on the Size and Distribution of the World's Christian Population." *Pew Research Center.*
https://www.pewresearch.org/religion/2011/12/19/global-christianity-exec
[185] Holy Trinity Brompton. https://htb.org
[186] Atherstone, Andrew. "Alpha Course will continue rebranding Christianity". *The Times.* https://www.thetimes.com/uk/article/alpha-course-will-continue-rebranding-christianity-whzxcp9fl
[187] Alpha. "Global Impact Study". *Alpha.* https://alpha.org.uk/global-impact-study
[188] Pike, David. "The Welsh Revival of 1904-5 - An Overview". *Welldigger.* https://daibach-welldigger.blogspot.com/2015/08/the-welsh-revival-of-1904-5-overview.html
[189] The UK population in 2022 was 67 million. *Macro Trends.* https://www.macrotrends.net/global-metrics/countries/GBR/united-kingdom/population

above, the number that could have been saved is similar to the Welsh Revival population saved percentage. The key difference is that the majority of those saved in the Welsh Revival was within 12 months whilst the Alpha attendance statistics are over c. 25 years.

The key point is that the gospel is still relevant in the UK as every year people attend courses like Alpha and become Christians. If more Christians joined Jesus in the harvest fields, more people would attend these courses, and more people would become Christians. If a larger number of Christians engaged with the Great Commission, the results could be truly significant.

The Engel Scale originates from James F Engel.[190] This scale is used to demonstrate that people go through a process and various decision-making steps on their way to conversion and spiritual maturity. This original model has been adapted by others, including the Evangelical Alliance: [191]

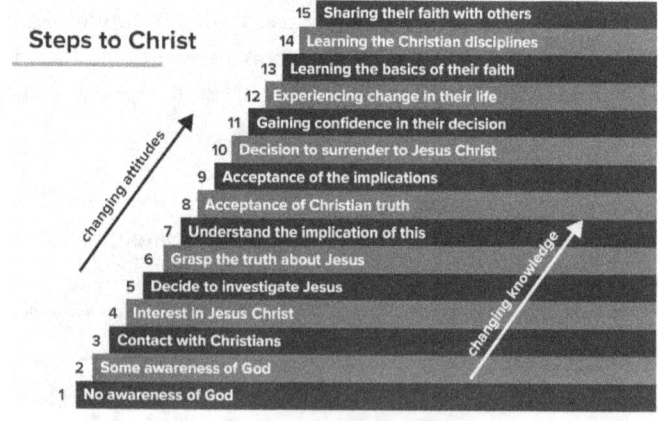

---

[190] Engel, James. *What's Gone Wrong With the Harvest?* Zondervan, 1975
[191] Evangelical Alliance. "What is the Engel scale?". *Evangelical Alliance.* https://www.eauk.org/great-commission/what-is-the-engel-scale

Some people may go along this journey quickly, whilst others can take many years. Recognising where non-Christian family, friends, neighbours, and work colleagues are on the scale can help us contextualise conversations about Jesus with them. Most non-Christians need regular positive interactions with Christians before they choose to follow Jesus.

The Engel Scale helps us contextualise our evangelism to where people are on their journey to faith. For example, if they are at stage 1 or 2 then our evangelism should focus on helping people encounter God so that they become aware of him. It may be unhelpful to talk about repentance until people reach step 8 which is at the point when they can consider the gospels' implications.

It is interesting to note that there is much debate amongst businesses about how many times you need to market to someone before they become a new customer. It started in the 1930s when the movie industry found through research that someone would need to see a movie poster 7 times before they would go to the cinema to see a movie.

This is now known as the effective frequency which is the number of times a person must be exposed to an advertising message before a response is made and before exposure is considered wasteful.[192] It is perhaps a little like choosing a marriage partner... Some people fall in love at first sight, but the majority of people need time to get to know each other before deciding to marry.

This highlights the need for more Christians to join Jesus in the harvest fields. The more Christians that are actively sharing their faith means that not only will more people be moving along the

---

[192] Marketing Dictionary. https://marketing-dictionary.org/e/effective-frequency

Engel Scale, they are also more likely to move through it sooner. Bringing people to salvation is usually a team effort, hence why we all need to engage.

Jesus highlights the importance of this salvation process:

> Don't you have a saying, "It's still four months until harvest"? I tell you, open your eyes and look at the fields! They are ripe for harvest. Even now the one who reaps draws a wage and harvests a crop for eternal life, so that the sower and the reaper may be glad together. Thus the saying "One sows and another reaps" is true. I sent you to reap what you have not worked for. Others have done the hard work, and you have reaped the benefits of their labour.
>
> John 4:25-38

The gospel is still relevant; it is a lack of harvest workers and contextualisation that are the problem. The gospel is as relevant today as it always has been. Training people how to share the gospel effectively in current Western culture and more Christians having the willingness to engage and to have confidence in their ability to make a difference, will impact the effective spread of the gospel.

Western society's current influences include identity politics, intersectionality and cancel culture.[193] Society is not affected as much by the postmodern worldview of enlightenment and relativism.[194] The evangelistic challenge for postmodernists was

---

[193] Merriam Webster. https://www.merriam-webster.com/dictionary/cancel%20culture; https://www.merriam-webster.com/dictionary/identity%20politics; https://www.merriam-webster.com/dictionary/intersectionality

[194] Britannica. https://www.britannica.com/topic/postmodernism-philosophy

the question – could Jesus Christ be the one objective truth for all humanity?

The evangelistic challenges for the current influences in Western culture are not the same as they were, so we need to ensure our evangelism approach is still relevant and not trying to answer questions people are no longer asking. We now live in a society where there are multiple ideologies, world views and voices.

Underpinning these multiple voices are fear-fuelled themes such as social breakdown, identity issues, diet, health, and climate change. Previous generations were influenced by grand narratives, whereas postmodernism questions these and society is now influenced by moral and factual relativism.[195] The result is that individuals in our society now define *their own truth*.

Therefore our approach to evangelism needs to change. It requires us to understand each individual and share the gospel in a way that is relevant to them. We do not compromise the gospel in any way but we need to share it in a way that answers the questions they are asking.

For example, what does Jesus want to communicate to those who adopt identity politics as their worldview? Maybe Jesus would say that all people are made in his image (Gen. 1:27) and that is where we derive our true identity and understanding of humanity. We are God's design, made in his image, and all are treasured and loved by him (Jn. 3:16).

Our common humanity is what unites us, rather than divides us. Attributes of our humanity such as race, gender, sexual orientation and social background are important but are not the

---

[195] Britannica. https://www.britannica.com/topic/ethical-relativism

basis of our identity.[196] Our true identity comes from being sons and daughters of God and our societal divisions can only be fully resolved by God and his children (Rom. 8:14-30).

What about those who define themselves by intersectionality? This sociological analytical framework defines how individuals' social and political identities result in unique combinations of discrimination and privilege. In short, they define their identities based on multiple types of discrimination they, their relatives or their forebearers have experienced.

Maybe Jesus would first want to validate any pain and trauma they will have experienced through multiple social factors of discrimination. The gospel communicates that Jesus took the impact of their discrimination to the cross, so they could live in freedom (Jn. 8:36). Maybe Jesus would say that their future is defined, not by *their* trauma, but by *his* trauma and death on the cross.

Cancel culture is defined as a "cultural phenomenon in which some who are deemed to have acted or spoken in an unacceptable manner are ostracized, boycotted, or shunned."[197] One of the core issues with cancel culture is that it sees forgiveness as a weakness because its followers believe it denies the seriousness of wrongdoing.

How far from the truth this is from Jesus' perspective! Jesus took sin so seriously that he chose to die for all wrongdoing and injustice (1 Jn. 2:2). The fact that Jesus took upon himself the penalty for sin so that we are forgiven for all our sins, means that we can forgive others (1 Jn. 1:9). This enables us not to judge or condemn, but instead forgive others (Lk. 6:37).

---

[196] The mystery of Christ is that all humanity are heirs together and members of one body (Ephesians 3:1-6)
[197] Wikipedia. en.wikipedia.org/wiki/Cancel_culture

These are just suggested starting points on how to evangelise to those who adopt the current thinking in our society. The key point is that the gospel is still relevant to Western society and the gospel can still transform lives. Spending time with non-Christians helps us understand what is important to them so we can share the gospel in a relevant way with them.

The harvest is ready

Jesus has told us that the harvest is ready. Do we believe this statement by Jesus and do we live like it is true? A survey in 2023 found that 74% of non-Christian students would go to church if they were invited by a friend. It also found that 73% said "yes" or "maybe later" to the question, "Would you like to hear the story of Jesus?"[198]

When Jesus was travelling and preaching through towns and villages, that was his perspective. He had compassion for people and saw that they needed help from God:

> Jesus went through all the towns and villages, teaching in their synagogues, proclaiming the good news of the kingdom and healing every disease and illness. When he saw the crowds, he had compassion on them, because they were harassed and helpless, like sheep without a shepherd.
>
> Then he said to his disciples, 'The harvest is plentiful but the workers are few. Ask the Lord of the harvest, therefore, to send out workers into his harvest field.'
>
> Matthew 9:35-38

---

[198] Stewardship. "Fusion: Engaging a spiritually open generation". *Stewardship*. https://www.stewardship.org.uk/stories/fusion-engaging-spiritually-open-generation

One of the core elements of evangelism is to see people through the eyes of Jesus' compassion. When we do so, we see their needs and are therefore also moved with compassion to help them. When Jesus preached and ministered to crowds, very few of them took issue with what he did or said. They often welcomed him and were amazed at his miracles.

At Capernaum, "they were amazed at his teaching, because his words had authority." (Lk. 4:32). When Jesus healed a paralysed man they said, "We have never seen anything like this!" (Mk. 2:12). Jesus has come to call sinners. We expect that most sinners will want him (Mk. 2:17).

The issue is often that we don't share a compelling gospel. For over 150 years the main way the church has been taught to do evangelism is based upon the methods used within the nineteenth Century revivals. These revivals were influenced by *Pragmatism*, which brought an over-emphasis on using methods to get results.[199]

Evangelistic methods such as praying the Sinner's Prayer were introduced by Charles Finney as a means to encourage a person to decide to follow Christ.[200]. He devised these methods based on his theology that repentance was a moral choice rather than a spiritual rebirth through the work of the Holy Spirit (Jn. 3:3).[201]

He therefore put sin, hell and repentance front and centre in his evangelism methods to encourage people to make a moral choice to change. Finney did not believe in Jesus' atonement on the cross for all our sin.[202] Despite his theology, the use of his

---

[199] Britannica. www.britannica.com/topic/pragmatism-philosophy
[200] Wikipedia. en.wikipedia.org/wiki/Sinner's_prayer
[201] Charles Grandison Finney. *Finney's Systematic Theology*. Bethany House Publishers, 1976
[202] Michael Horton. "The Disturbing Legacy of Charles Finney". *Monergism*.
https://www.monergism.com/disturbing-legacy-charles-finney

methods have become a template for sharing the gospel in churches, missions and crusades across the world.

These methods can encourage unbelievers to make decisions, regardless of whether they are ready to become a Christian. Some research has shown that on average only 6% of people who pray a sinner's prayer at evangelistic events, join a church and the majority do not become disciples.[203]

Theologian Shawn Brace states that "Finney's methods inherently objectify people, stripping them of their humanity, they actually counter-work the very all-of-life disciple-making journey the mission of Jesus requires".[204] Evangelism should lead to discipleship, not just conversion.

The other impact of these methods is that some Christians can find them clunky. When they try and follow the method, it doesn't work for them. Consequently, they may conclude unhelpfully that they are not any good at sharing their faith. This can then lead them to disengage from talking about Jesus with non-Christians and not participating in evangelistic initiatives.

Mark Greene, author and Mission Champion at the London Institute for Contemporary Christianity (LICC), writes "There is a danger in trying to systematize anything as mysterious as evangelism, a danger in reducing it to ten principles or seven keys... as if there is a magic formula. It smacks of manipulation. And is something to be wary of. Nevertheless, when we are learning something, it can be helpful to have a framework. Ultimately it gives us freedom".[205]

---

[203] Myers, Jeremy. "Is Crusade Evangelism Effective?". *Redeeming God*. https://redeeminggod.com/crusade-evangelism-effective

[204] Brace, Shawn. "The "Anxious Bench" and Our Preoccupation with Numerical Growth" *Reimagining Faith*. https://shawnbrace.substack.com/p/the-anxious-bench-and-our-preoccupation

[205] Greene, Mark. Fruitfulness on the Frontline: Making A Difference Where You Are. IVP, 2014.

Another issue with method-based approaches is that they are not the approach that Jesus used. Jesus taught about and helped unbelievers find the treasure of the Kingdom of God so that they will give all they have to obtain it.

> The kingdom of heaven is like treasure hidden in a field. When a man found it, he hid it again, and then in his joy went and sold all he had and bought that field.
>
> Again, the kingdom of heaven is like a merchant looking for fine pearls. When he found one of great value, he went away and sold everything he had and bought it.
>
> Matthew 13:44-46

Jesus' message was a gospel of his kingdom, it wasn't just about sin and repentance. If we consider the messianic prophecies about Jesus, they include a suffering servant and a triumphant king.[206] Jesus' gospel is about his suffering *and* his kingship. If we only preach about repentance we are missing half of Jesus' message.

The emphasis on evangelism should be on helping unbelievers experience the reality of Jesus and his kingdom. Non-Christians often need to experience Jesus' kingdom multiple times before they repent. As they begin to realise how amazing Jesus is, and that he can transform their lives, they will choose him.

We may think people are not interested in the gospel because they may have a poor response to a partial gospel message. If we help people experience the riches of Jesus's kingdom, they are more likely to respond to him. Before we decide whether

---

[206] Examples are Isa. 53 and Zec. 9:9

people are interested in Jesus or not, we first need to show them all that Jesus is.

John Finney's book *Finding Faith Today* is one of the most recent in-depth, large-scale empirical examinations of how people in the UK respond to the Gospel. His research shows that the majority of people in the UK (69%) come to faith through a gradual process rather than a sudden crisis moment conversion.[207]

Such statistics underline and support Jesus's approach to introducing the reality of his Father and kingdom to people as a motivation for repentance. Offering to pray for someone that their circumstances change, or for them to experience Jesus personally, or his healing, or his voice or his peace, can go a long way towards them becoming a follower of Jesus.

The recent Talking Jesus Research Report in the UK shows that the majority of non-Christians consider Christians that they know to be caring (50%) and friendly (62%). For non-Christians who had a conversation with a Christian, 75% felt comfortable during the conversation and 36% were open to an experience or encounter with Jesus.[208]

These statistics suggest that we are potentially pushing on an open door when it comes to sharing Jesus with people around us. This statistic also challenges the viewpoint that the harvest is not ready. It may be time to rethink our perspectives on the harvest, how to do evangelism and people's openness to the gospel.

---

[207] Finney, John. *Finding Faith Today: How Does It Happen.* Bible Society, 1996.
[208] Talking Jesus. "2022 Research Report". *Talking Jesus.* https://talkingjesus.org/research

Jesus describes evangelism as an organic process, based on how a farmer sowed his seed:

> A farmer went out to sow his seed. As he was scattering the seed, some fell along the path, and the birds came and ate it up. Some fell on rocky places, where it did not have much soil. It sprang up quickly, because the soil was shallow. But when the sun came up, the plants were scorched, and they withered because they had no root. Other seed fell among thorns, which grew up and choked the plants. Still other seed fell on good soil, where it produced a crop – a hundred, sixty or thirty times what was sown.
>
> Matthew 13:3-8

Jesus is saying that we should share the gospel widely with all types of people, whether we think they will respond positively or not. This is our responsibility – much like a farmer, they have to trust that the soil will cause the seeds to grow. In the same way, we have to trust God that as we sow seed, he will make it grow.

Also, note that the plants in the soil sprang up quickly, which was not a good thing as they had no roots and died. Evangelism is an organic process and shouldn't be rushed. We need to sow into people's lives by talking about Jesus and introducing people to his kingdom over a period of time before the fruit can be harvested.

Your invitation from Jesus is to join him in the harvest fields and work alongside him. We need to be committed to the harvest cycles of heaven – sowing, watering and reaping. We may not reap what we have sowed because "one sows and another reaps" (Jn. 4:37). Harvesting can be hard work but together we can harvest a crop for eternal life (Jn. 4:36).

If you want to explore the importance of the kingdom gospel in further detail, we would recommend our Book *God's Dream: Our Greatest Privilege* and our course *Developing A Spirit-led Evangelistic Lifestyle (DASEL)*.[209] We also have additional resources that discuss this topic on our blog.[210]

Jesus invites you to fish for people

When Jesus started inviting people to follow him, he invited two fishermen called Peter and Andrew to follow him. Jesus said to them "I will send you out to fish for people." (Mt. 4:19). Traditionally this has been translated as "fisher of men" but the Greek word anthrōpos is not gender specific, so includes both men and women.[211]

Interestingly, Jesus uses this language with fishermen, so they would understand the analogy that Jesus is using for unsaved people. It is also worth noting that in an Old Testament prophecy about sin and restoration, Jeremiah uses the language of fishermen and hunters (Jer. 16:1-16).

From ANE perspective, which is mirrored by Old Testament authors, the sea is often regarded as a place of chaos that God brings to order (Gen. 1:10).[212] This is why the sea looks like glass in Heaven, it is a picture that God has stilled all chaos and disobedience (Rev. 4:6). With this worldview, it would have

---

[209] God's Dream – Our Greatest Privilege. www.evangelismreimagined.org/books; *The DASEL Course*. www.evangelismreimagined.org/courses
[210] Gilpin, Mark & Fiona. "What is Jesus' gospel?". *Evangelism Reimagined*. https://www.evangelismreimagined.org/what-is-jesus-gospel
[211] anthrōpos, Strong's G444
[212] The Bible Project. "Chaotic Waters". *The Bible Project*. https://bibleproject.com/podcast/series-h2r-p21-metaphor-e3-chaotic-waters

been significant for the disciples to see Jesus calm the storm when they thought they might drown (Mk. 4:35-41).

The image here is of fishing for people from a chaotic domain of sin and death to bring them into the Kingdom of God so they can be reconciled to God and know his peace. Fishing is the Biblical image of how we save people. The keys to successful fishing are the right location, gear and bait – along with patience.

When God invites you to fish, he knows the best places for you to go and the best gear to use. We don't have to blindly go anywhere to fish or use any method in the hope that we may catch something. We can learn to be led by Jesus, in the same way as the disciples were, with the miraculous catch of fish (Lk. 5:1-11).

As with most sports, fishing is an art as much as a science, it takes practice to gain confidence. As with other things in life, we can give up through disappointment at the lack of results. What is needed is a growth mindset that enables us to develop resilience whilst we learn.[213] All of us can grow in our ability to fish for people.

Jesus, who came to seek and save the lost, is an amazing teacher and coach who can show us how to apply our unique strengths to fishing.[214] He can also help us develop a mindset to help us sustain an evangelistic lifestyle.[215] For most of us, it will take some time to learn how to consistently fish for people.

---

[213] Wiktionary. https://en.wiktionary.org/wiki/growth_mindset
[214] Gilpin, Mark & Fiona. "God has uniquely designed you to be evangelistic". *Evangelism Reimagined*. https://www.evangelismreimagined.org/god-has-uniquely-designed-you-to-be-evangelistic
[215] Gilpin, Mark & Fiona. "Sustaining an evangelistic lifestyle". *Evangelism Reimagined*. www.evangelismreimagined.org/sustaining-an-evangelistic-lifestyle

JESUS AMOUNG THE LOST

As we spend time fishing for people, we will catch Jesus' heart and compassion for the lost. We will also feel the approval of Father God as we, his children, are drawn into the family business of seeking and saving the lost. The Holy Spirit can also reveal the secrets of unbelievers' hearts, so they can see God in us (1 Cor. 14:24-25).[216]

If we want more of God, then we need to follow him and go where he is, which includes joining him among the unsaved (Jn. 12:26). Will you regularly invest time to be with unbelieving family, neighbours, colleagues and strangers? Will you develop an evangelistic lifestyle so that seeking and saving the lost becomes part of who you are and a high priority in your life?

Connor Doll from YWAM says "When we engage our hearts with God's, we can't help but become part of the solution."[217] When we spend time in worship and prayer it is natural for us to embody Jesus's desires and priorities. Jesus invites you on your greatest adventure to seek and save the lost - will you join in?

Evangelist Billy Graham said, "The highest form of worship is the worship of unselfish Christian service. The greatest form of praise is the sound of consecrated feet seeking out the lost and helpless". The more of God that we seek will be found among those who don't know him.

Will we go and find Jesus among the lost?

---

[216] Strongs G2588, the soul or mind, as it is the fountain and seat of the thoughts, passions, desires, appetites, affections, purposes, endeavours, character, stirred in a bad way or good.
[217] Youth With A Mission. ywam.org

Reflection

Consider these verses:

> *From that time on Jesus began to preach, 'Repent, for the kingdom of heaven has come near.' As Jesus was walking beside the Sea of Galilee, he saw two brothers, Simon called Peter and his brother Andrew. They were casting a net into the lake, for they were fishermen. Come, follow me,' Jesus said, 'and I will send you out to fish for people.' At once they left their nets and followed him.*
>
> Matthew 4:17-20

Ask Father God:

- Lord, have I got any hindrances to sharing my faith that need to be dealt with?
- Lord, how do you see me intentionally sharing my faith with unbelievers around me?
- Lord, how can I get equipped so I can learn how to seek and save the lost?

Prayer:

> *Thank you for inviting me to work in the harvest fields with you. Help me make this a priority in my life and to learn how to fish for people. Show me who around me is nearer to the kingdom than I think they are so I can know where to start.*

To do:

- Spend some time reading Bible stories where Jesus draws unbelievers to him, so you can learn how he did evangelism.
- If you have family and friends that are not Christians ask Jesus to send harvest workers to them.
- Ask Father God to help you discover your evangelistic strengths.

Further reading:

- Luke 7:31-35
- Genesis 15:1-5
- Revelation 7:9-12

JESUS AMONG THE MARGINALISED

"There are many callings, but none higher than to give water to the thirsty and food to the hungry."
(Rolland Baker, Missionary & Author)

Pure religion

If you were asked to define pure religion, how would you define it? Would you include in your definition love for Jesus, being righteous, obeying the Bible, and keeping the Ten Commandments? These are all important points, but the apostle James goes further:

> Do not merely listen to the word, and so deceive yourselves. Do what it says. Anyone who listens to the word but does not do what it says is like someone who looks at his face in a mirror and, after looking at himself, goes away and immediately forgets what he looks like.
>
> But whoever looks intently into the perfect law that gives freedom and continues in it – not forgetting what they have heard but doing it – they will be blessed in what they do.
>
> Those who consider themselves religious and yet do not keep a tight rein on their tongues deceive themselves, and their religion is worthless. Religion that God our Father accepts as pure and faultless is this: to look after

orphans and widows in their distress and to keep oneself from being polluted by the world.

James 1:22-27

Western culture often centres around individualism, self, and reasoning.[218] This means, at times, we do not think holistically and collectively as much as Eastern people tend to. We can even think about something abstractly without any lived experience. We can even kid ourselves that we have done something just because we thought about it!

James rightly discounts this, meaning we are not righteous based only on our thoughts, but also on our actions. We can't just talk about the needs of the poor and marginalised and then not do anything about it. We also can't leave it to someone else to do; James does not give us that option.

Jesus also makes it clear what our responsibilities are to both God and other human beings:

> "Love the Lord your God with all your heart and with all your soul and with all your mind." This is the first and greatest commandment.
>
> And the second is like it: "Love your neighbour as yourself." All the Law and the Prophets hang on these two commandments.

Matthew 22:37-40

---

[218] Robson, David. "How East and West think in profoundly different ways". *BBC*. https://www.bbc.com/future/article/20170118-how-east-and-west-think-in-profoundly-different-ways

These two commandments are the foundation for our lives – love God first, then love people. It is not one of these, it's both; we can't focus solely on one and neglect the other. True Christianity requires us to love both God and the people he has created. If we love God, then we have to love what is important to him – people.

If we pour out our heart in genuine love and emotion towards God during sung worship and yet ignore the lost, poor and marginalised, then there is something incomplete or wrong in our hearts, minds and faith. Is a Christian someone who professes belief in Jesus or someone who follows Jesus in how he thinks, speaks and acts?

The apostle James says:

> Suppose a brother or a sister is without clothes and daily food. If one of you says to them, 'Go in peace; keep warm and well fed,' but does nothing about their physical needs, what good is it? In the same way, faith by itself, if it is not accompanied by action, is dead.
>
> James 2:15-17

In the chapter *Christ In Us*, we explored what it meant for Jesus to come and make his home in us. This means we get the opportunity to learn what is important to Jesus, what are his priorities and how to love him well. If we think it is just about how Jesus loves me and how I love him, then we have missed the fact that we need to learn also to love others well.

Jesus' summary of the law sums up what is most important to him. It is not a preference or a good idea, it flows from the core of his being, helping us see what Jesus' clear priorities are.

Key questions for us are

    1. Do we recognise this?
    2. Will we make space in our lives for it?
    3. Will we turn it into practical action?

The Kingdom of God

When Jesus ascended to heaven he was given an everlasting kingdom (Dan. 7:9-14). Jesus' message was about the gospel of the kingdom (Mt. 24:14). He spoke about and demonstrated the reality and nearness of his kingdom (Mt. 4:17 & Mt. 15:30). It was the focus of Jesus' teaching, he used twenty-five parables to describe it. [219]

The kingdom that came with Jesus was written about in the Old Testament by prophets, it was what some of the Jews of Jesus' day were looking for.[220] Yet the fulfilment of these prophecies was different from what some of the Jews expected (Mk. 6:14-15). Some of them expected a military leader like King David (Isa. 11:1).

After being in the wilderness, Jesus began to teach in synagogues in Galilee and then he went to Nazareth where he had grown up. Whilst he was there, he read part of two messianic prophecies:

> He went to Nazareth, where he had been brought up, and on the Sabbath day he went into the synagogue, as was his custom. He stood up to read, and the scroll of the prophet Isaiah was handed to him.

---

[219] Bible Study Tools Staff. "The Parables of Jesus". *Bible Study Tools*. https://www.biblestudytools.com/topical-verses/parables-of-jesus
[220] For example, Simeon, Lk. 2:25-35

Unrolling it, he found the place where it is written:

> 'The Spirit of the Lord is on me, because he has anointed me to proclaim good news to the poor.
>
> He has sent me to proclaim freedom for the prisoners and recovery of sight for the blind, to set the oppressed free, to proclaim the year of the Lord's favour.'

Then he rolled up the scroll, gave it back to the attendant and sat down. The eyes of everyone in the synagogue were fastened on him. He began by saying to them, 'Today this scripture is fulfilled in your hearing.'

Luke 4:16-21

Here, by referencing Isaiah 58 and 61, Jesus is explaining what his kingship and kingdom looks like. As we explained in the chapter *Jesus In The Bible*, we can understand that whilst Jesus is only quoting three verses, his audience would understand he is referring to several messianic prophecies in Isaiah.

To help us understand the full weight of what Jesus is saying we need to consider not only the words he is using but also what he is referring to in the messianic prophecies. This then provides us with a greater understanding of an important aspect of what his kingdom entails.

When Jesus says in Luke 4:18 "The Spirit of the Lord is on me, because he has anointed me to proclaim good news to the poor", he is referring to Isaiah 61:1,2. To understand what Jesus means here we need to consider both what John and Isaiah wrote.

In Luke 4:18, "the poor" means those destitute of wealth, influence, position, learning, and honour and those who are powerless, helpless, and needy.[221] The word translated "poor" in Isaiah 61:1, which Jesus is referencing, means humble, weak, lowly and afflicted.[222]

When Jesus says in Luke 4:18-19 "He has sent me to proclaim freedom for the prisoners and recovery of sight for the blind, to set the oppressed free, to proclaim the year of the Lord's favour", he is referring to Isaiah 58:6. This passage powerfully describes the importance and blessings of helping the poor and oppressed.

In Luke 4:18, "prisoner" means a captive or prisoner of war, and "oppress" means to break, shatter and smite.[223] In Isaiah 58:6 "oppress" means to crush or break.[224]. Jesus' focus on the poor includes both those who are suffering as a result of their own actions and those as a result of the actions of others.[225] Regardless, Jesus' agenda for both is freedom.

From a W.E.I.R.D. perspective, the nation-state provides laws and support to protect and help the marginalised. From an ANE perspective, it was the extended family's responsibility to do this. So if you were excluded from the extended family because you became orphaned, widowed or divorced, you were on your own without help.

---

[221] ptōchos, Strong's G4434
[222] ānāv, Strong's H6035
[223] aichmalōtos, Strong's G164; thrauō, Strong's G2352
[224] rāṣaṣ, Strong's H7533
[225] The term 'marginalised' has been applied to those on the edge of society since the 1920's. Where the Bible uses the word 'poor', today we would think of economic, political, social, and cultural marginalisation.

This is one reason that Jesus prioritised these marginalised people. When he was teaching and doing miracles, he included them. He did not seek fame, affirmation of others or prioritise mixing in elite circles. Jesus mixed with and spoke directly to marginalised people; he made time for them.

Examples included Jesus speaking with, having compassion for and healing lepers, shamed women, ignored children, and beggars.[226] Jesus defined his kingship by saying "the blind receive sight, the lame walk, those who have leprosy are cleansed, the deaf hear, the dead are raised, and the good news is proclaimed to the poor." (Mt. 11:5).

It is also worth noting who the angels appeared to after the birth of Jesus. It was to shepherds that the angels announced the good news that the Messiah had been born (Lk. 2:8-14). In Jesus' day, shepherds were considered to hold the lowest profession possible in society. They were nearly always ceremonially unclean due to their job and therefore could not go to the temple to worship.[227]

Jesus is clear that we are to love our neighbour as ourselves and show mercy to people, even those we don't like or find difficult. When Jesus told the story about the Good Samaritan, he used a Samaritan as the hero, who helped the Jewish person who was attacked by robbers (Lk. 10:25-37). In Jesus' day, the animosity of the Jews and Samaritans meant they did not mix.[228] Jesus was using a person from an intensely disliked people group to challenge their racist attitudes.

---

[226] Mk. 1:41-42, Jn. 4:1-26, Mk. 10:13-16 and Lk. 18:35-43
[227] They would often be ceremonially unclean. Thomas, Geoff. "Learning from the shepherds". *Evangelical Times.* https://www.evangelical-times.org/learning-from-the-shepherds
[228] Samaria would have been located in modern-day Palestine

A rich man, whom Jesus loved, was challenged by Jesus to sell everything he had to give to the poor because money, possession and wealth cannot be more important than Jesus and his kingdom (Mk. 10:17-29). Jesus tells us directly to sell our possessions and give to the poor and invest instead in heavenly treasure (Lk. 12:32-34).

In the Old Testament, God is described as a father to the fatherless and a defender of widows (Ps. 68:5). Proverbs also tells us that if we oppress the poor we show contempt for God, but whoever is kind to the needy honours God (Prv. 14:31). Proverbs also tells us that the righteous care about justice for the poor and whoever is kind to the poor lends to God (Prv. 29:7 & Prv. 19:17). God identifies himself here with the poor. The way we treat the poor is a reflection of how we treat God. Profound!

We cannot separate who Jesus is, what he achieved on the cross, his seeking and saving the lost, his discipleship of men and women, his teaching and miraculous healing outside of having compassion for the marginalised. Jesus has not left this option open to us. If we are to follow him, then our actions towards the marginalised will mirror his.

It is a core part of Jesus' kingship. It is who he is and what he cares about. Jesus did not ignore or overlook the marginalised. He did this, not only because he cared about them, but also because he wanted to show us it is a priority for him and as an example for us to follow.

The sheep and the goats

Jesus uses three parables to help us understand how we will be judged – the parable of the ten virgins, the parable of the bags of gold and the parable of the sheep and goats (Mt. 25:1-46). These parables challenge us to how to live so that we will be judged well instead of realising too late that we gave greater importance to earthly priorities than heavenly ones. [229]

The parable of the sheep and goats focuses on what we should have done but didn't do:

> 'When the Son of Man comes in his glory, and all the angels with him, he will sit on his glorious throne. All the nations will be gathered before him, and he will separate the people one from another as a shepherd separates the sheep from the goats. He will put the sheep on his right and the goats on his left.
>
> 'Then the King will say to those on his right, "Come, you who are blessed by my Father; take your inheritance, the kingdom prepared for you since the creation of the world. For I was hungry and you gave me something to eat, I was thirsty and you gave me something to drink, I was a stranger and you invited me in, I needed clothes and you clothed me, I was ill and you looked after me, I was in prison and you came to visit me."
>
> 'Then the righteous will answer him, "Lord, when did we see you hungry and feed you, or thirsty and give you something to drink? When did we see you a stranger and invite you in, or needing clothes and clothe you? When did we see you ill or in prison and go to visit you?"

---

[229] Commentaries differ in their understanding of these parables. For example, some theologians think the Parable of the ten virgins represents either being unprepared, being a hypocrite, not having the Holy Spirit or not showing enough mercy.

'The King will reply, "Truly I tell you, whatever you did for one of the least of these brothers and sisters of mine, you did for me."

'Then he will say to those on his left, "Depart from me, you who are cursed, into the eternal fire prepared for the devil and his angels. For I was hungry and you gave me nothing to eat, I was thirsty and you gave me nothing to drink, I was a stranger and you did not invite me in, I needed clothes and you did not clothe me, I was ill and in prison and you did not look after me."

'They also will answer, "Lord, when did we see you hungry or thirsty or a stranger or needing clothes or ill or in prison, and did not help you?"

'He will reply, "Truly I tell you, whatever you did not do for one of the least of these, you did not do for me."

'Then they will go away to eternal punishment, but the righteous to eternal life.'

Matthew 25:31-46

The focus of this parable seems to be – have we loved our neighbour as we loved ourselves? So if we were hungry, thirsty, naked or in prison, we would want people to provide for us and visit us. As Micah stated "What does the Lord require of you? To act justly and to love mercy and to walk humbly with your God." (Mic. 6:8).

What is potentially most surprising is who Jesus identifies with in this parable. He does not identify with those who are helping or ignoring the marginalised, rather he *identifies with the marginalised.* Jesus implies that is it personal to him whether the marginalised are helped or ignored.

Jesus identifies with those who are hungry, thirsty, lonely, naked, ill and those in prison. The sheep are those who responded to these needs but did not realise that in their actions they were ministering directly to Jesus. The goats are those that did not respond, or have any concern for them, and did not see Jesus among the marginalised.

This is a significant challenge for us because if we ignore people in need, Jesus implies that we are directly ignoring him. "Brothers and sisters" in Matthew 25:40 can mean natural siblings, belonging to the same people group or a fellow believer.[230] This is potentially because he is implying he regards the marginalised as his brothers and sisters.

When Paul went to Jerusalem to validate the gospel he was preaching, the other apostles asked: "that we should continue to remember the poor, the very thing I had been eager to do all along." (Gal. 2:10). Having been with Jesus, the apostles knew how important it was to look after the poor.

When we spend time with Jesus, his heart for the poor should rub off on us. It is not a question of whether we should help, it is a question of how and who should we help. Helping the marginalised is an essential and powerful way of being like Jesus. John Chrysostom, an early church father, warned, "If you cannot find Christ in the beggar at the church door, you will not find him in the chalice.".

---

[230] adelphos, Strong's G80

How do we engage with the marginalised?

There are many ways to engage with the marginalised but the most important step can often be the first one. It is starting the journey that matters, even if we feel out of our depth and do not know whether we can make a difference. Remember that Jesus is among the marginalised and we will be finding him there.

Jesus' plumbline for loving others is to love them as we love ourselves (Mt. 22:37-40). When we see someone in need, we should ask ourselves how would we like to be loved if we were in their situation? When we understand how we would like to be loved, then we can love the marginalised person in that way.

We were visiting a city and were taking in the sights. We turned a corner and we spotted a woman begging for money on the street. She was old, only had one hand and was visibly uncomfortable sitting on the pavement. Our hearts were moved with compassion to help.

We discussed what we could do and decided to go to a nearby café and buy her some food for lunch. We then approached her and offered her the food and drink we had purchased. She was visibly moved and had tears in her eyes when we handed it over. We were unable to have more of an interaction with her because she didn't speak English.

There are probably lots of reasons why this woman was in this position. There will most likely be a back story that we will have involved difficulty and pain. The majority of people we meet who are homeless or begging have had difficult lives or trauma that caused them to break in some way. It is a myth that people choose to be homeless.[231]

Marginalised people can have complex needs, but at the moment when you meet them, they may have basic needs. They may need food, encouragement, someone who listens, a bus fare, a warm coat, or a prayer for healing. Whatever these simple needs are in the moment, they are not usually beyond any of us to meet them.

We regularly buy food for people who are homeless that we may come across whilst we are out and about. We may also stop and sit with them whilst they eat their food and we may listen as they tell us their story. We may not be able to solve all their needs at the time, but that does not mean we should not love them as best we can in that moment.

The reality is that the majority of us have some time, energy, wisdom, ability and resources to help the marginalised around us. When John the Baptist was asked what they should do in response to his message, the first thing he said was "Anyone who has two shirts should share with the one who has none, and anyone who has food should do the same" (Lk. 3:11).

John's response was highly practical and not beyond what was possible for his audience. He was saying we should share some of what we have with them. Most of us will have spare clothes that we can give away to specific people or a charity. Many of us can give some of our food away, it is within our means to help.

---

[231] YMCA. "Myth busting: 5 common homelessness myth". *YMCA*.
https://www.ymcadlg.org/myth-busting-homelessness-myths

We are to help those in need inside and outside the church because Jesus asks us to invite the unsaved poor and marginalised into his kingdom. Jesus' kingdom and church are places where those with practical needs have them met, otherwise, as the apostle James says "faith by itself, if it is not accompanied by action, is dead." (Jas. 2:17).

Jesus' parable about the wedding banquet highlights his desire for the marginalised to be part of his kingdom:

> When one of those at the table with him heard this, he said to Jesus, 'Blessed is the one who will eat at the feast in the kingdom of God.'
>
> Jesus replied: 'A certain man was preparing a great banquet and invited many guests. At the time of the banquet he sent his servant to tell those who had been invited, "Come, for everything is now ready."
>
> 'But they all alike began to make excuses. The first said, "I have just bought a field, and I must go and see it. Please excuse me."
>
> 'Another said, "I have just bought five yoke of oxen, and I'm on my way to try them out. Please excuse me."
>
> 'Still another said, "I have just got married, so I can't come."
>
> 'The servant came back and reported this to his master. Then the owner of the house became angry and ordered his servant, "Go out quickly into the streets and alleys of the town and bring in the poor, the crippled, the blind and the lame."

"'Sir,' the servant said, "what you ordered has been done, but there is still room."

'Then the master told his servant, "Go out to the roads and country lanes and compel them to come in, so that my house will be full. I tell you, not one of those who were invited will get a taste of my banquet."'

Luke 14:15-24

Jesus' kingdom is so different to Western society that favours the rich, famous, gentry, influential and intelligent. It is not that these people are not invited into his kingdom, because they are, but some will turn him down. Because of this, the king's response was to invite the poor, the crippled, the blind and the lame.

This parable is also included in Matthew's gospel and it ends with Jesus saying, "for many are invited, but few are chosen" (Mt. 22:14). As Matthew's gospel was primarily written to a Jewish audience, Jesus is likely saying that gentiles and not just Jews are invited. The point here is that the gospel is to be taken to everyone, regardless of their place in society, cultural background or religious heritage.

It is our collective responsibility to help those in need. We can help the marginalised by giving our time and money to charities that focus on the marginalised. We can also help our neighbours, families, friends, work colleagues and strangers. None of us can help everyone, but between us all, we can help many.

Our responsibility to the marginalised is both individual and collective. We can help someone we meet ourselves but we can also come together to make a greater impact. For example, there is a charity called Gravesham Sanctuary that improves the life outcomes for people experiencing homelessness in Gravesend.[232]

Churches in Gravesend were grasped by a vision "that no one should be homeless on their watch." They have worked together for a decade and throughout this time have got many people off the streets and prevented homelessness for others. Many have been signposted to drug and alcohol services and others have been helped to tackle their relational and material poverty. The charity also runs a six-bed HMO and a daily drop-in centre. [233]

Hundreds of volunteers have provided 50,000 hours of help. They have served over 15,000 meals and prevented over 5,000 rough sleeps. This has also resulted in over 170 people being rehoused. Some of those helped have become Christians and joined local churches. This is not something unique to Gravesend, but similar initiatives are run by multiple churches across the UK.

How big is the need?

Research shows that there are over 300,000 homeless people in England, of which 140,000 are children.[234] 18% of people in the UK are in absolute poverty after housing costs due to low incomes and 7.2 million people are in households with food insecurity.[235]

---

[232] Gravesend Sanctuary, https://www.graveshamsanctuary.uk
[233] HMO stands for "House in Multiple Occupation" and is primarily a UK property term, referring to a residential property where multiple, unrelated households share common areas like kitchens and bathrooms.
[234] Shelter. "At least 309,000 people homeless in England today". *Shelter.* https://england.shelter.org.uk/media/press_release/at_least_309000_people_homeless_in_england_today
[235] Francis-Devine, Brigid. "Poverty in the UK: Statistics (2024)". *House of Commons.* https://researchbriefings.files.parliament.uk/documents/SN07096/SN07096.pdf

The number of people in the UK leaving the workforce due to long-term sickness is at its highest since the 1990s and claims for government health benefits have risen 68% between 2020 and 2024.[236] The workforce in the UK is taking more sick days than at any point in the last decade.[237]

The Mental Health of Children and Young People in England 2023 report, published by NHS England, found that 20.3% of 8 to 16-year-olds had a probable mental disorder in 2023. Among 17 to 19-year-olds, the proportion was 23.3%, while in 20 to 25-year-olds it was 21.7%.[238]

About 7% of UK children have attempted suicide by the age of 17 and almost one in four say they have self-harmed in the past year.[239] Over 250,000 children and young people were admitted to hospital in 2023 as a result of self-harm.[240] Tragically, there are even some websites providing access to graphic content, and details about methods of harm.[241]

One in four women, one in six children and one in eight men in England and Wales have been raped or sexually assaulted. In 2023, the research found that 97% of women aged 18-24 have

---

[236] Masud, Faarea. "Sick people leaving workforce at record highs". *BBC News.* https://www.bbc.co.uk/news/business-68639144

[237] Sri-Pathma, Vishala. "Sick days at work hit highest level for 10 years". *BBC News.* https://www.bbc.co.uk/news/business-66883087

[238] NHS England. "One in five children and young people had a probable mental disorder in 2023". *NHS England.* https://www.england.nhs.uk/2023/11/one-in-five-children-and-young-people-had-a-probable-mental-disorder-in-2023

[239] UCL. "Mental ill-health at age 17 in the UK". *UCL.* https://cls.ucl.ac.uk/wp-content/uploads/2020/11/Mental-ill-health-at-age-17---CLS-briefing-paper---website.pdf

[240] Nuffield Trust. "Hospital admissions as a result of self-harm in children and young people". *Nuffield Trust.* https://www.nuffieldtrust.org.uk/resource/hospital-admissions-as-a-result-of-self-harm-in-children-and-young-people

[241] The Samaritans. "How social media users experience self-harm and suicide content". *The Samaritans.* https://media.samaritans.org/documents/Samaritans_How_social_media_users_experience_self-harm_and_suicide_content_WEB_v3.pdf

been sexually harassed.[242] In 2021 the UK government invested five million pounds to twenty-two organisations to improve the safety of women and girls.[243]

More than a third (36%) of UK adults report experiencing workplace discrimination, which includes discrimination based on age, gender, disability, race and sexuality.[244] A report in 2022 revealed that 75% of women of colour experienced racism at work.[245] When it comes to bullying at work 29% of workers will experience it and 47% have observed it.[246]

These are just some of the needs in the UK. If you live in another country you can usually find out statistics about a nation's needs by looking at government departments who usually publish annual reports about what they are doing to help. Also, non-governmental organisations (NGOs) undertake and publish research.

People can be marginalised because of a variety of issues, as UK Aid Match helpfully defines:

> Marginalisation describes both a process, and a condition, that prevents individuals or groups from full participation in social, economic and political life. As a condition, it can prevent individuals from actively participating. There is a

---

[242] UN Women. "Public Spaces Need To Be Safe And Inclusive For All. Now". *UN Women UK*. https://www.unwomenuk.org/safe-spaces-now

[243] UK Government. "Millions awarded for new projects to keep women safe". GOV.UK. https://www.gov.uk/government/news/millions-awarded-for-new-projects-to-keep-women-safe

[244] Ciphr. "Workplace discrimination statistics in 2021". *Ciphr*. https://www.ciphr.com/infographics/workplace-discrimination-statistics

[245] Fawcett. "Landmark Report Reveals 75% of Women of Colour Have Experienced Racism at Work". *Fawcett*. https://www.fawcettsociety.org.uk/news/landmark-report-reveals-75-of-women-of-colour-have-experienced-racism-at-work

[246] Maskell, Rachael. "Bullying and Respect at Work (2023). *UK Parliament*. https://hansard.parliament.uk/commons/2023-07-11/debates/7435C28E-7F68-4747-BD9C-EDCA0824B2AD/BullyingAndRespectAtWork; Psychiatry UK. "Workplace bullying: What is it? And how do we stop it?". *Psychiatry UK*. https://psychiatry-uk.com/workplace-bullying-what-is-it-and-how-do-we-stop-it

multidimensional aspect, with social, economic and political barriers all contributing to the marginalisation of an individual or group of individuals.

People can be marginalised due to multiple factors: sexual orientation, gender, geography, ethnicity, religion, displacement, conflict or disability. Poverty is both a consequence and a cause of being marginalised. However, policy makers do not consider that all forms of marginalised or poorest populations have equal weighting, that there are different levels of poverty and marginalisation within each context.

There are core factors that determine who or what groups are marginalised and what the barriers are that prevent them from being reached. Political discrimination may marginalise some ethnic groups, migrants or regions of a country. Social discrimination and marginalisation can impact on a wide range of groups based on age, gender, sexuality, language or disability. Economic marginalisation can prevent equal access to basic services, income opportunities and access to jobs.[247]

What are the needs in your community and who are the most marginalised? Why not partner with an organisation that is addressing this need? Find a list of relevant charities or a directory of charities. For example, multiple anti-trafficking organisations are helping to prevent modern slavery.[248]

If we look back to the start of the Salvation Army in the nineteenth century, they lived out a practical Christianity to

---

[247] UK Aid Match. "Defining marginalised – the Foreign, Commonwealth & Development Office's 'Leaving no one behind' agenda". *UK Aid Match.* https://www.ukaidmatch.org/wp-content/uploads/2020/10/Defining-marginalised-leave-no-one-behind.pdf

[248] Evangelical Alliance. "Anti-slavery groups". *Evangelical Alliance.* https://www.eauk.org/current-affairs/politics/modern-slavery/anti-slavery-groups.cfm

encourage both social and spiritual transformation of society's most vulnerable and marginalised people. For them, being a Christian included helping those in most need in society. It was not an optional extra.[249]

150 years on, the Salvation Army is at work in more than 130 countries. Their first projects in the UK included shelters for people who were homeless, a family tracing service, running soup kitchens, helping people who were living in slums and setting up rescue homes for women fleeing domestic abuse and prostitution.

There are now hundreds of Christian charities engaged in helping the marginalised and tackling causes of marginalisation. But what about you and your church? How are you and they helping the marginalised in your local area? All our churches can contribute to the needs of society.

There are many worship songs today that encourage us to engage with Father God to know his ways and his heart. The inference can be that an encounter will help us know who God is and his priorities. Whilst this can be helpful, the Bible already tells us the marginalised are a priority for God, especially the fatherless and widows.[250]

If we want to know God's heart and be close to him, then it will mean taking on the important things that are in God's heart – his love for people, his desire for justice, his desire for us to co-labour with him to help the marginalised. How can we encounter our heavenly Father in sung worship without being profoundly impacted by what is important to him?

---

[249] The Salvation Army. "Our History". *The Salvation Army*.
https://www.salvationarmy.org.uk/about-us/our-history
[250] For example, Isaiah 1:17, Psalm 82:3, Deuteronomy 10:18 and James 1:27

When missionary Jackie Pullinger was at a conference in the UK with over four thousand attendees, the band were encouraging the attendees to cry out to God for more of him in their lives. Jackie was agitated and went on stage to share her thoughts. She said "I hear you crying out to the Lord, asking him for more. But your problem is that you are on the wrong diet."

Jackie then went on to explain that if we want more of God, we will find him in the act of service among the poor. She made the point that discovering more of God is not so much about asking him to bless our desires but aligning our longings with his desires. It's about finding out what he is doing and having the courage to join in.

Missionaries who are active amongst the lost and marginalised understand this. Rolland Baker says "To us missions is the natural outworking of our faith. It is the way we return the love God has for us. There is no other option. Revival without missions is deficient. To turn away from the lost, poor and needy is to turn away from God."

It may at times be difficult and discouraging

Whilst God works profoundly amongst the world's marginalised, their situations can be complex because of the trauma and lack of family stability, access to resources and opportunities in their lives. Few of them will be able to access treatments that would help them resolve the physical, emotional and psychological healing they need.

Therefore their path to health and integration into society may not be straightforward; it may have multiple setbacks and relapses. If we love and support these people, when such moments occur we may feel hurt, disappointed and discouraged. At these times it is helpful to remember it is about them, not us, and that God can share his patience and kindness with us (Rom. 2:4).

We may have helped someone in the past who turned their back on us or we may feel we were taken for a ride and the person was seeking their needs to be met without any desire to change. This can leave us once bitten and twice shy, and we then may withdraw from helping others.

When we were in our twenties we were enjoying a day in London together and whilst we were there we came across an older lady searching through the litter bins for food. I (Fiona) thought that it was awful that this woman was looking in a bin to find food. So as I had an apple in my bag, I offered it to her.

At this point, she seemed to be offended by my offer of the apple and she started loudly swearing at me. The noise of her voice attracted the attention of people around me and I felt so embarrassed that I walked away from her. This incident impacted me deeply and I sadly stopped engaging with homeless people for several years because of it.

God is not like us in this regard, as he is faithful and keeps "his covenant of love to a thousand generations of those who love him and keep his commandments" (Deut. 7:9). We may need to develop resilience when we are helping the marginalised so that we can truly represent God to them.

It is also ok when we don't know how to best help some people or when they don't want to accept help. If we take a long-term viewpoint, we can focus on being the best help that we know how to be in the moment. We don't have to think that we have all the answers, it is often a team effort that is required.

Steve's story

We first met Steve when we were serving food to the homeless and those on the edge of society in our town. He was young, funny and full of energy, but sadly struggled with an alcohol addiction. He was in a regular cycle of alcoholism which meant it was hard to maintain a job and meaningful relationships. He had so much life in him and the potential to live life to the full.

It was heartbreaking to see Steve's life circling downwards. We would see him regularly and try to engage him about the root of his alcoholism, but he did not want to talk about it. We would present Jesus as the answer to his pain and a new future life. Another member of the team offered to help find him a rehab place.

Eventually, he broke the law and ended up in prison. Whilst there he had treatment for his alcoholism and also attended an Alpha course in prison.[251] Although his time in prison was not easy, he broke his addiction to alcohol and started to realise that God was real and cared for him. He started to think about a different life.

When we next saw Steve he was a different person. He was well-kempt, sober and still funny. He shared about his experience in prison and also, to our surprise, recounted past conversations word for word that we had had with him about Jesus, even though he was drunk at the time.

A few months later he became a Christian and started a new life following Jesus. Steve is someone that Jesus makes time for because no one is beyond his redemption. Even though his

---

[251] The Alpha Course runs in more than 400 prisons and secure facilities, in 30 countries. *Run Alpha.* https://alpha.org.uk/prisons

situation was complicated and his destination unclear, Jesus wants us to join him in reaching out to people like Steve.

The marginalised often have complex stories and needs that may at times need specialist help. However, a team effort from multiple Christians over a period of time can make a significant difference. The key question is will we prioritise our time to help the marginalised using the skills and life experience we have?

If you are wanting more of God, spend time with the marginalised, Jesus is waiting for us to find him there.

Reflection

Consider these verses:

> *The Spirit of the Lord is on me, because he has anointed me to proclaim good news to the poor. He has sent me to proclaim freedom for the prisoners and recovery of sight for the blind, to set the oppressed free, to proclaim the year of the Lord's favour.*
>
> Luke 4:18-19

> *As the Father has sent me, I am sending you.*
>
> John 20:21

Ask Father God:

- Lord, will you share your heart with me for the poor and marginalised?
- Lord, who in my local neighbourhood could I help?
- Lord, is there a charity or cause that I could give my money and time to?

Prayer:

> *Thank you that you care about the marginalised and that you invite them into your kingdom. Help me to make this a priority in my life and learn how to help those in need.*

Connect me with people that have the same heart and concern as I do, so that I can work with them to make a difference.

To do:

- Spend some time with God asking him about his heart for the poor and the marginalised.
- Think about causes that you care about and which one matters to you most.
- Research charities that work in the area that you care about and consider how you can best support them.

Further reading:

- Isaiah 58:1-14
- Psalm 82:3-4
- Acts 9:36-43

REMAINING IN JESUS

Be with Jesus. Become like him. Do as he did.
(John Mark Comer, Author and Pastor)

Clutter distracts us from more important things

We live in a time where there is the danger of being overloaded with information, with competing demands for our time and attention and digital apps that are purposely designed to get and hold our attention.[252] Add to this the normal demands of life and dealing with our internal worlds; we may be anxious, struggling to forgive, discouraged, feel unloved, damaged through trauma or just plain busy.

Yet living a life where we think, speak and act like Jesus is within our grasp; it is the life that Jesus invites us into when he asks us to follow him. Jesus is realistic about how possible it is, but also about how much we may or may not prioritise him. We get to decide how much more of him we really want.

Accepting the invitation to follow Jesus is the most profound and most important choice we can ever make. It affects our eternal destiny and reward (1 Cor. 3:11-14). Yet how often are we distracted by competing emotions and desires? We can so easily settle for an easy life and routinely ask God for more in our lives without actually pursuing it.

---

[252] Center for Humane Technology. "The Attention Economy - Why do tech companies fight for our attention? *Center for Humane Technology*. https://www.humanetech.com/youth/the-attention-economy

Within all of this, God wants us to know him, his passions and his priorities. He invites us into an intimate relationship where our lives are characterised by finding him within ourselves, in the Bible, and amongst other believers, the lost and the marginalised.

If we want more of him, then simply asking through prayer and song is not enough if it does not result in us *changing our lives* to fit his passions and priorities. It may be time for a reality check as to what is most important to us and whether we are following Jesus casually or wholeheartedly.

We should not ignore or overlook any desire in us for more of God; such desire is God-given. Therefore we should respond to his invitation and journey with God by following him to all the places he is. This is *the way* we get more of God (Jn. 12:26). Our capacity for him grows as we join in with what he is doing.

To make this possible, we will need to deal with any unwanted internal clutter to make space for Jesus' thoughts, motivations and desires. This is not just about our wellbeing, it is also about changing our internal world to align with how Jesus thinks and feels. To know him well will involve sharing in his joys, passions and sorrows.

If we don't address our internal clutter we will not be able to make space for Jesus. Despite our attempts to follow him, our internal clutter will hinder us from reaching our desired goal. We can try and follow Jesus more wholeheartedly but if our internal world is not in order, we are unlikely to make any significant progress.

If we learn to remain in Jesus and in his love, he and his love remains in us, then our lives will be fruitful (Jn. 15:1-17). Through this, we become his friends, know his joy, experience his love, treasure his words, keep his commands, and let him prune us so we can become more fruitful. The challenge is that this is a lifelong journey without any shortcuts and quick fixes.

It is a relational journey. We get the opportunity to invest in our relationship with Jesus. As we do this, Jesus moulds us to be like him so that we make time for what is important to him. As is usually the case with any long-term investments, the return is greater than short-term investments.

The most prudent way to invest financially is typically to invest every week or month so that your money grows over time despite the ups and downs of financial markets and inflation. It is similar to our relationship with Jesus, we need to make regular investments in our relationship with him by making time in our lives to be with him and follow him.

It is unusual that it is solely one moment or encounter with Jesus where everything will be put right, yet our personal and church practices may give the impression that there is. Jesus presents a very different approach, one where we are invited into a discipleship-based relationship where we need to learn to be faithful with what he gives us (Lk. 16:10).

We shouldn't fall for the illusion of spiritual shortcuts any more than we should for the get-rich-quick schemes. They promise much but are ultimately misleading despite their appeal. We simply cannot live in the fullness of God without changing our lives to pursue a relationship with Jesus and his priorities.

God's fullness in Jesus is our example

Jesus is our *primary example* of what it looks like to live a life that has all the fullness of God (Col. 1:19 & 2:9). If we want more of God in our lives, our lives need to look like Jesus' life. There is no escape or alternative to this truth, if we want more of God then our lives have to centre around what Jesus said and did.

When we talk about becoming a Christian we often use the phrase "ask Jesus into your life", yet Jesus' discipleship is about him inviting us into a life that mirrors his – on the inside and outside. It is not about us striving in our strength to do more for God, it is about learning to abide in him and him changing us into his likeness (2 Cor. 3:18).

As we have explored, this is not about simply asking him for more but is primarily about putting his words into practice (Mt. 7:26). We can spend our time seeking more of God through ways other than what he has given us and get discouraged. We can also mistakenly think there may be something wrong with us, when in fact it is our method that is wrong.

If we align our priorities and passions with him and join him where he is, we will experience the fullness of God that we desire. This does not mean having a hectic life, but rather making space for all that Jesus cares about. We get to willingly choose his priorities and make them our own.

Pastor and author John Wimber said, "Show me where you spend your time, money and energy and I'll tell you what you worship." [253] As we start to make Jesus' priorities our own they will start to affect how we spend our time, money and energy. If we truly worship Jesus, we will make space in our lives for what is important to him.

Jesus does not seem to give us the choice to pick and choose which of his priorities we think we should adopt. He has not given us this option, any more than he has given us an option

---

[253] Wimber, John. *Power Healing*. HarperOne, 2009.

to sin in some ways and not others. Jesus will challenge us about anything that gets in the way of us following him.

For example, in the story of the rich young ruler, he rejected Jesus and instead chose his wealth (Mt. 19:16-30). Jesus respected his decision and did not chase after him saying that he should reconsider. This story shows us that if we do not choose Jesus' priorities, it does not mean he will chase us down to persuade us to reconsider whether we want more of God or not.

Another example is Jesus' parable about the good Samaritan (Lk. 10:25-37). Through the parable Jesus challenges the expert in the law, as well as ourselves, to not try and minimise our responsibility by having a narrow definition of who our neighbour is. Jesus was clear this includes people we most dislike and our enemies.

Jesus also leads by example, showing us that his priorities include reaching the lost and helping the marginalised. Though these at times can be hard they are often the most rewarding. We cannot say we are truly loving and representing Jesus if we ignore these two priorities of his.

Experiencing the fullness of God is not just a personal pursuit but also that of the church, which requires all Jesus' gifts to mature us so that we can all reach unity in faith and knowledge, and therefore attain "to the whole measure of the fullness of Christ" (Eph. 4:13). By loving each other, his love can become complete in us (Phil. 2:2, Col. 2:2 & 1 Jn. 4:17).

Within a Western culture that elevates individualism, we may think we can reach maturity and live in the fullness of God on our own, but that is not how he has designed it. We need each other and we need to journey together, as our collective fruitfulness will be much greater than our individual efforts.

Our relational journey towards the fullness of God is not just with Jesus but with each other. As we learn to serve each other in the context of Jesus' passions and priorities, it makes space for God to do more among us. Jesus describes a unity that shows the impact of these symbiotic relationships:

> My prayer is not for them alone. I pray also for those who will believe in me through their message, that all of them may be one, Father, just as you are in me and I am in you.
>
> May they also be in us so that the world may believe that you have sent me. I have given them the glory that you gave me, that they may be one as we are one – I in them and you in me – so that they may be brought to complete unity.
>
> Then the world will know that you sent me and have loved them even as you have loved me.
>
> John 17:20-23

Jesus prays to his Father "You are in me and I am in you" and then "I in them and you in me". It is these individual and collective symbiotic relationships that will lead to the fullness of God. God loves to dwell in individuals, groups of Christians, local congregations and the world-wide church, which is part of his strategy to make himself known to every human being on the planet.

The stakes are high – will we make space in our daily lives for more of God and follow him to the places where he is, so that the world will know who he is? Our lives have the potential to positively impact so many people, but that requires us to "pay the most careful attention, therefore, to what we have heard." (Heb. 2:1).

True discipleship

True discipleship is to spend time with Jesus so that we become like him and do what he does (Jn. 8:31-32). This is the only way to get more of God and live in the fullness of God. We need to renew our minds and put Jesus' words into practice (Rom. 12:2 & Mt. 7:24-27). The goal is to align our internal and external worlds with his priorities rather than our own.

If we are followers of Jesus then Jesus will be first in our lives. Evangelist J. John uses this acrostic of FIRST: "Is he first in my Finances, is he first in my Interests, is he first in my Relationships, is he first in my Schedule and is he first in my Troubles? If we can say he is first my finances, interests, relationships, schedule and troubles, then that is a good sign that he is first."

At their live farewell show in London, the band Delirious? played many of their greatest hits, but they also left this challenge to the audience:

> "Fabula este vestry, the Latin says the story is yours. This is not the end, but this is a fantastic beginning. The people movement of history makers that goes on and on and on.
>
> You know people, I am calling you to stand up, to stand up, for we are the people on this planet right now, we must stand up. It is time to be men and women of God."

We only get one life, and for most of us, it will be in our hearts to want to make a difference. So will we stand up and stand out as true disciples of Jesus? Paul says, "For the creation waits in eager expectation for the children of God to be revealed". (Rom 8:19). The more we become like Jesus, the more the world will get to see what he is truly like.

Jesus said, "I have come that they may have life, and have it to the full." (Jn. 10:10). Here, "full" means exceeding, abundant, more than is necessary, superior, extraordinary and remarkable.[254] This is the life that Jesus offers to us all, a life that he lived, and a life that he modelled for us.

He showed us what living in the fullness of God looked like, which is a life he wants us to replicate. We can experience much of what Christianity offers, but we do not want to miss its meaning – that we are to learn to think, speak and be more like Jesus. To do this we must make space for him in our cluttered lives and join him in the places where he is.

When we pray and ask for more of God, he wants to give us something more profound – *his fullness*. He wants us individually and collectively to become like him by forming Christ in us (Gal. 4:19). Have we made it about a better life, more money, a growing ministry, greater influence or a bigger platform?

More of God is about becoming a disciple of Jesus. It is both our privilege and responsibility to become disciples of Jesus. He has designed it this way and it is the only way we can attain to his fullness. So let us all go on the journey collectively and individually to think, speak and be like Jesus.

---

[254] perissos, Strong's G4053

It's probably best summed up by the Apostle John:

> We know that we have come to know him if we keep his commands. Whoever says, 'I know him,' but does not do what he commands is a liar, and the truth is not in that person.
>
> But if anyone obeys his word, love for God is truly made complete in them. This is how we know we are in him: whoever claims to live in him must live as Jesus did.
>
> 1 John 2:3-6

Will we clear out our clutter, seek his fullness, make his priorities our priorities and become true disciples of Jesus?

A Prayer

Make my life a prayer to you, I wanna do what you want me to. No empty words and no white lies, no token prayers, no compromise.

I wanna shine the light you gave, through your Son you sent to save us from ourselves and our despair, it comforts me to know you're really there.

Well I wanna thank you now for being patient with me, oh it's so hard to see when my eyes are on me.

I guess I'll have to trust and just believe what you say, oh you're coming again, coming to take me away.

I wanna die and let you give your life to me so I might live and share the hope you gave me, the love that set me free.

I wanna tell the world out there you're not some fable or fairy tale that I've made up inside my head. You're God the Son and you've risen from the dead.

Amen.

Make My Life a Prayer to You, Keith Green.

www.ingramcontent.com/pod-product-compliance
Lightning Source LLC
Chambersburg PA
CBHW071953070526
44583CB00015B/1182